TRAIN UP YOUR CHILD

Inspiration and Insight for Today's Christian Parent

Train Up Your Child

Inspiration and Insight for Today's Christian Parent

by
Chuck Sturgeon

Harrison House
Tulsa, Oklahoma

Train Up Your Child
Inspiration and Insight for Today's Christian Parent
ISBN 1-57794-159-4
Copyright © 1998 by Chuck Sturgeon
P. O. Box 904
Enid, Oklahoma 73702-0904

Published by Harrison House, Inc.
P. O. Box 35035
Tulsa, Oklahoma 74153

Dedication

It would only be fitting to dedicate this book in the Spirit to the Lord Jesus Christ for without Him I can do nothing. **I am the vine, ye are the branches: He that abideth in me, and I in him, the same bringeth forth much fruit: for without me ye can do nothing** (John 15:5).

Also in the Spirit this book is dedicated to my family. No one person outside of Jesus has so changed my life than my sweetheart Dea. From the first day I met her only my love for Jesus could be greater than my love for her. As a wife, mother and grandmother, she is truly a "virtuous woman." Proverbs 31:10-31 describes her in every way: **...but a woman that feareth the Lord, she shall be praised** (Prov. 31:30b). She loved me into the kingdom.

My three sons and their families are a delight to me. Mike is our "Joseph," taking any situation to end up prospering and leading with confidence. Brian is of the tribe of Judah ("praise"), and Shane is a lover. Our "daughter-in-loves" are so precious, and the grandchildren—it would take another book to describe how wonderful they are.

To my mother, Pearl, a woman of prayer; to my late father, Bud, who you'll read about in this book, a true daddy.

In conclusion, to Lloyd and Dorothy Galusha, my in-laws who stood and prayed the prayer of agreement with Papa Hagin (Kenneth E. Hagin) in the late 60's and claimed my salvation and baptism in the Holy Spirit.

Contents

Foreword

When I first discovered Chuck Sturgeon's book, I immediately recognized it as a powerful revelation from the heart of God. It was particularly important to me because of God's calling on my life. I was eager to work with children and could hardly wait to grow up, marry and have a family of my own.

Today, I minister to thousands of children around the world and have four of my own. So I know the pressures they face. I also know they are spiritually hungry. They long to have God's Word spoken over them and demonstrated in front of them.

That's why I use Chuck's book in my ministry and in my home. I teach from it, I parent by it and I give copies of it to others. Why? Because **godly parenting works!** It has helped me raise my own children, and I've seen it help others. Especially those who are experiencing challenges with their children.

That's why I encourage you to do more than just read this book. Study it. Get this revelation in your heart and speak it out of your mouth. Let your children see your faith in action on a daily basis. As you do, you'll reap the rewards of one of God's most powerful promises, "Train up a child in the way he should go: and when he is old, he *will not* depart from it." (Proverbs 22:6)

Kellie Copeland
Eagle Mountain International Church
and Kenneth Copeland Ministries
Fort Worth, Texas

Acknowledgments

In 1971, a husband and wife team with great tenacity brought a Bible course on reel-to-reel tapes to my house, and through their efforts and the work of the Holy Spirit, I was saved, delivered, received the baptism of the Holy Spirit and renewed my commitment to the call of God on my life that I had received at the age of nine. Lawrence and Isabelle Ward both are receiving their heavenly rewards.

The Bible Believer's Course was Kenneth Copeland's, and we cut our spiritual teeth on such messages saying, "If God can do it for Kenneth and Gloria, then He can do it for us." And He did! Thank you, Kenneth and Gloria, for putting your sermons on tape.

Also at this time we were introduced to the ministry of U. L. Harshfield who then pastored the Church of the New Life in Oklahoma City. It was 80 miles one way for us to hear his teaching and take in the special speakers, but it was worth every mile. Thank you U. L. and Gerry for your foresight and vision to minister to others.

Next we started working in a local Assembly of God church pastored and founded by Rev. John Morgan. "Brother John," as we affectionately called him, taught us by example. Such a man of prayer he was, and he pastored the whole community regardless of where you attended church.

What a gold mine we found in Papa Hagin's (Kenneth E. Hagin's) tapes, books, seminars and campmeetings. Wow! We could tell even Kenneth Copeland had learned from him. This ministry helped shape and mold our lives and still does. Bless you, Papa Hagin!

All of the above have had a great impact on our lives. We also want to thank Julie Dawn Filson who worked days putting our first manuscript together, *Train Up a Child*, and the Harrison House staff and editors for putting this one together and making me look good.

Tiny Hands

Never mind that my hands are small
Or how tiny my fingers may be.
God works through only willing hearts
And there is none as willing as me.

You see, even I can lay hands on the sick —
And they recover! My prayers are fervent too.
I can help, comfort and deliver
Because my faith is strong and true.

So please don't doubt God's power in me
Or think that I don't hear from above,
'Cause God looks on the inside of a child,
And to Him, I'm a giant of love!

Jana Hancock
Meno, Oklahoma

GOD'S PLAN: THE FAMILY

Many homes today are a study in chaos. Tempers often flare as parents yell at their children and children yell at their parents.

Too many children rule the home with their incessant whining and threats of rebellion as their parents give in to avoid another confrontation. These parents often live a life of fear, dreading what their children will do next. Meanwhile, their children run the gamut of drugs and sex, "looking for answers in all the wrong places." Ultimately, these parents and their children may become the victims of broken homes, ruined reputations and misdirected lives.

But that is *not* God's plan. He wants families to prosper as every family member obeys His commandments and serves Him in harmony. He wants the home to be a place of peace, comfort, refuge and safety — a place of joy, happiness and love.

The Importance of the Christian Home

The Christian home is extremely important to the heart of God. He knows that the devil can't run our nations, our states, our counties or our provinces unless he first destroys the Christian home.

Therefore, as parents, we need to recognize that our occupation or ministry should never take precedence over our families. God has set up a divine order. Our relationship with Him comes first, and our family comes second. We can only be successful in life and ministry as we place our homes in that divine order.

I once looked at that word H-O-M-E and thought of the phrase "**H**elping **O**thers **M**inister **E**ffectively." That's what a successful Christian home is supposed to do. In fact, the best way for pastors to achieve unity in their churches is to help the families in their congregations find unity within their homes. But that will only happen as family members begin to *do* the Word, not just *hear* it.

Proverbs 1:7 says, **The fear of the Lord is the beginning of knowledge: but fools despise wisdom and instruction.** According to that Scripture, if parents don't accept and obey the Word's instruction regarding their ministry in the home, they are fools!

So where do we as parents start in learning how to fulfill our "home ministry"? According to Proverbs 1:7, we start by developing a reverential fear of God in our lives and in our children's lives. He is the Almighty God. He is El Shaddai, the God who is more than enough, the great Provider.

As we obey God in reverential fear, He will make our families strong. He will perfect that which concerns us (Ps. 138:8). He will cause those desires in our hearts regarding our families to come to pass.

Revival Starts in the Home

Malachi 4:5-6 reveals the importance God places on the family.

> **Behold, I will send you Elijah the prophet before the coming of the great and dreadful day of the Lord:** *And he shall turn the heart of the fathers to the children, and the heart of the children to their fathers, lest I come and smite the earth with a curse.*

Then in Luke 1:17, we see the fulfillment of this passage of Scripture in Malachi. Along comes a baby who will grow up to be John the Baptist! And the angel tells Zacharias that his son will go before the

Messiah **in the spirit and power of Elias, *to turn the hearts of the fathers to the children,* and the disobedient to the wisdom of the just; to make ready a people prepared for the Lord.**

Notice what comes first: the hearts of the father are turned to the children. You see, revival starts in the home.

When parents turn their hearts toward obeying God's Word and fulfilling their responsibilities to each other and to their children, the power and anointing of God begins to rest upon them. They earn their children's respect as the children come to recognize that Mama and Daddy hear from God.

You see, children see parents as they really are. And if the parents act like Brother and Sister Goody Two-Shoes when they go to church on Sunday and then live like hell the rest of the week, their children just aren't going to listen to them!

But once the hearts of the parents are turned toward their children in godly love and discipline, then things begin to change in the home. Even when their children are disobedient, they eventually come and ask the wisdom of the just — the wisdom of those who are righteous and who know the right direction to take. In other words, the children begin to listen to their parents!

This is the kind of Christian home where revival starts. A home in God's divine order helps to make ready a people prepared for the Lord.

The Sturgeon Story

My wife Dea and I have traveled for many years teaching on the home and family. But there was a time in our lives when our marriage was a total mess and our lives were just falling apart.

Nine years after Dea and I were married, I began to drink. I became an alcoholic, on my way to hell. We also began to have terrible financial problems. My wrong decisions got the family so deeply in debt, we could look up and still not see the bottom! Snakes would have a higher place to crawl!

We had creditors calling us day and night. The financial pressure, plus my excessive drinking, began to break up our marriage. We fought constantly, cutting each other down, hurting each other, destroying the love that we had for each other. Dea decided there was no other way out of the mess but to divorce me.

But God began to speak to Dea's heart, and she began to return to the God of her youth. Dea knew God could work miracles. She had been born again at the age of nine and raised in a Pentecostal church where, as a child, she had seen miracles. So when the Lord said to her, "I have a better way than divorce," Dea took that as a "rhema" word from God specifically for her situation. She began to seek God earnestly for her family.

Dea prayed in tongues for me several hours a day for almost three months. As she interceded for me, things began to change.

One of the first times Dea saw a sign of the change taking place inside me was the day I came home and cleaned out my liquor cabinet. I told her, "I just can't drink in this house." I didn't know why that was so, but Dea did. She had been filling our home with praise and worship, changing the whole atmosphere in the house!

But my life was still in a mess. So one day, I picked up my loaded .38 special handgun, cocked back the hair trigger and pointed it at my head. I was ready to end it all.

I heard a voice tell me, "Go ahead. It will all be over." But then another voice said to me, "Put the gun down." I knew the second voice was the voice of the Lord. So very carefully, I lowered the gun from my head and put it down.

Five days later, an elderly husband-and-wife ministry team visited our house and introduced us to some teaching tapes of Kenneth Copeland. By the time I finished listening to the second tape, I was ready to get saved and filled with the Spirit. My life was totally turned around from that time on.

As Dea had prayed in the Spirit, she had become actively involved in the spirit realm, loving me into the kingdom of God. Through it all, she had ministered to my spirit, to my soul and to my body even when I didn't deserve it. She started treating me as if I were already saved and taking my place as the spiritual head of the house when I was still acting like a heathen.

Thank God for women who will stay with it and never give up praying for their husbands and their families! Love works!

I have fallen so much in love with my wife over the years since then. I thank God that Dea didn't leave me when it looked hopeless. I don't think I would be here today if she hadn't stood by my side.

It is so precious to have a sweetheart who was willing to believe God for me and stand with me. I salute her for that. I know when we get to heaven, she will receive rewards for her fight of faith to save her family.

Well, Dea and I began to grow together in the Lord. Over the years, we learned how to live by biblical principles in our husband-and-wife relationship and in training our children. Then God thrust us forward to teach other couples the same principles on the home and family that we had learned through the Word and our own experiences. Why? Because He is interested in helping the Christian family!

It Is Worth It All

When I was an alcoholic, I had tried to drown my troubles in a bottle, but the problems would be floating on top the very next morning! There finally came a time when I watched everything I owned get repossessed. I lost everything I had inherited. I even signed away the portion of the ranch and farm my father had given to me!

I lost it all — but after I gave my life to Jesus, He eventually helped me get it all back.

Parents, it's worth it for us to stand in faith for our families. It's worth it for us not to give up until we have established a godly home.

I know what it's like to be down at the bottom with my home life a total mess — and I am not going back! I have found out what it's like to have children who will hug you and love on you. Even to this day, when I walk into the store where my grown son works, he will drop anything he is doing and give me a hug right in front of all of his fellow employees. My other two sons are the same way — and my wife gives me more than hugs!

Does my family love me like that because I'm such a good fellow? No, God is just a very good God! He turned our family around, and He will do the same for you!

The Importance of a Child

If God is that interested in the Christian home, how much importance does He place on the children in a home?

We can answer that question by looking at what Jesus said in Matthew 18.

> **At the same time came the disciples unto Jesus, saying, Who is the greatest in the kingdom of heaven?**
> **And Jesus called a little child unto him, and set him in the midst of them, And said, Verily I say unto you, Except ye be converted, and become as little children, ye shall not enter into the kingdom of heaven.**
> **Matthew 18:1-3**

Jesus used a child as an example of someone who is the greatest in the kingdom of heaven. He said, "Unless you become as little children, you cannot enter the kingdom of heaven" (v. 3). What did Jesus mean by that? Well, think about how a child forgives so simply and quickly and with such purity. Children are much more trusting and loving than most adults.

For instance, two children may argue and say mean things to each other at school one morning. But before school is out that day, they will probably have their arms around each other and be best pals again! And they will treat each other as if they never did anything wrong.

Now, if it was *our* son or daughter involved in the situation, we might want to go tell the other parents what their child did to our child. Then the principal and the school board might find out about the problem, and before long, we would really have a fight on our hands! Meanwhile, the two children have already forgiven each other and are happily playing together again!

So who is the greatest in the kingdom of heaven? Jesus picked up a little child and said, "Except you become as a little child, you shall not enter the kingdom of heaven."

Now, if you still don't think children are very important to Jesus, read on in Matthew 18 to see what else He says about them.

And whoso shall receive one such little child in my name receiveth me.

Matthew 18:5

If you receive a little child, it's just like receiving Jesus Himself! Isn't that a wonderful truth for mamas and daddies and anyone else who takes care of children?

On the other hand, verse 6 shows how Jesus feels about anyone who would stumble the faith of a little child.

> **But whoso shall offend one of these little ones which believe in me, it were better for him that a millstone were hanged about his neck, and that he were drowned in the depth of the sea.**
>
> Matthew 18:6

Then in Matthew 18:10, Jesus made another intriguing statement about children:

> **Take heed that ye despise not one of these little ones; for I say unto you, That in heaven their angels do always behold the face of my Father which is in heaven.**

Jesus says here that children have their own angels who behold the face of the Father in heaven. Well, does that mean that once children grow up, they don't have their angels anymore?

No, Jesus was only stressing that angels watch over children just as much as they watch over adults. Children are little people, no less important in God's eyes than adults! And Jesus warned us to take heed that we don't despise one of these little ones.

Children are also important to the heavenly Father. Jesus said in Matthew 18:14, **Even so it is not the will of your Father which is in heaven, that one of these little ones should perish.** It is vital that parents give their children the Word of God and train them in the way they should go. God doesn't want anyone to go to hell.

Of Such Is the Kingdom of Heaven

Jesus had more to say about little children in Matthew 19:13-14:

> **Then were there brought unto him little children, that he should put his hands on them, and pray: and the disciples rebuked them. But Jesus said, Suffer little children, and *forbid them not, to come unto me: for of such is the kingdom of heaven.***

First the disciples rebuked the adults — the parents, aunts, uncles or grandparents — who brought the children. But then Jesus rebuked the disciples, saying, "No, let the little children come unto Me, for the kingdom of heaven is made up of such as these."

Is heaven literally made up of little children? No, I believe that Jesus was explaining that in the spirit realm, there really is no difference between a child and an adult. Both children and adults are three-part beings — spirit, soul and body.

So in essence Jesus was saying, "As far as I'm concerned, children are little people. They are spirit beings just like you adults are. So don't forbid them. Don't hinder them. Don't restrain them from coming unto Me!"

Jesus' rebuke to His disciples lets us know that we should never restrain or forbid our children from pursuing spiritual matters.

Some denominations believe that a child can't get saved or filled with the Holy Spirit until he or she is at least twelve years old. But God doesn't put an age requirement on receiving His gifts. In fact, some children receive revelation knowledge of the things of God much more easily than many adults do!

Lay Hands on Your Children and Pray

Then Jesus laid hands on the children, praying for them and blessing them. There must be a good reason why Jesus laid hands on the children to pray for them. Evidently, something is imparted in the realm of the Spirit through the laying on of hands.

Therefore, we as parents should learn from Jesus' example and regularly lay hands on our children and pray for them. (Of course, if our children are older and have moved away from home, we can still confess the Word over them and pray for them. The arm of the Lord isn't shortened. He isn't limited by distance or time.)

It's also good when you lay hands on your children to pray in tongues. When you pray in tongues for someone, it's like shooting lightning bolts toward him in the Spirit to help him see himself as he really is.

Think of a person out in a storm who is trying to reach the safety of a nearby house. He isn't sure which way to go; it's dark, and he can't see the light of the house. Then suddenly, lightning streaks across the sky, and for just a split second he can see the path that will take him to safety.

That's what praying in tongues will do for your children in the spirit realm. As you pray in the Spirit for them, you'll send spiritual lightning bolts their way to help them see the right path to take. It is an effective way to pray for your children, and it will help cause things to start falling in line in their lives.

Children: The Church's Priority

We've seen how important children are to God. They are a high priority to Him. That's why the priority of the church should also be its children. For example, churches always offer meetings designed especially for adults. But services especially for children should also be offered.

Some pastors have the attitude, "Well, someday we want to start a children's church. Someday we want to set up a nursery and organize a youth group." But those should be the first priorities the church focuses on!

Why? Because the world's priority is your children. It produces all sorts of things (like all that worldly music we don't want our children listening to!) to try to lead them down the wrong path.

Even retail stores place a high priority on children. You may have to hunt to find a light bulb in a store, but the bubble gum is right next to the cash register where the cashier takes your money! And right on cue, your child will tug on your sleeve, begging, "Oh! Oh! I want that!"

A church that neglects its children will end up with children who neglect the church as they grow up. And a church won't succeed if it only tries to "hot dog" its teenagers to heaven. What do I mean by that? Well, it's fine to plan hot dog barbecues or pizza parties for the youth. Young people need social activities that they can enjoy with other Christian youth. But a church body's fellowship together — whether as adults or as teens or as little children — should ultimately be centered around the Word of God.

As a parent, you must recognize that the devil also places a high priority on your children. You and your spouse may be saved and filled with the Holy Ghost. You may like to attend teaching seminars in order to learn more and mature in the Lord.

But if you're not careful, while you're concentrating on your own spiritual growth, the devil will focus on tempting your children to do whatever their flesh wants to do. The enemy thinks, *I hate the Word that is in the parents — but just let me have their children, and I'll be able to hurt the whole family!*

So make the training of your children in the ways of the Lord a top priority in your life, and tap into God's plan for your family. In His eyes, a successful household is one where the man of the house is fulfilling his ministry as a husband and father. It's a home where the woman is a godly wife and mother. And it's a home where both parents are raising children to be godly seed in the earth!

WHY IS GODLY DISCIPLINE SO IMPORTANT?

One of the most important aspects of raising up godly seed on this earth is the proper disciplining of your children. Without godly discipline based on God's Word, children are left to flounder in life, following the inclinations of their own flesh nature.

Mistakes in Raising Children

Many times parents end up training their children according to the way their parents raised them instead of looking to the Word.

You may not even like the way Mom and Dad treated you. But I guarantee you, unless you receive revelation knowledge from God's Word to change the way you respond to situations, you are going to treat your children the same way your parents treated you.

Here's a common scenario: Two young, single adults who are making plans to marry tell each other, "Boy, I tell you what — we'll never raise our children the way our parents raised us!"

Then this couple gets married, and the children start coming along. Well, the young parents haven't been taught in church how to raise their children with godly discipline. The only knowledge they have to draw from is their experience of how they were raised.

So one or both of them begin to reason, *Well, I did live like the devil for a long time. I was hell on wheels! But now I'm doing all right; I didn't turn out too badly. I guess the way Mom and Dad disciplined me worked out after all. So I'm going to raise my kids the same way Mom and Dad raised me.*

But here is one thing you can be sure of: If Mom and Dad didn't discipline them according to the Word of God, that couple is going to have problems in raising their children!

Then there are a lot of parents who may want to raise godly children, but they aren't living godly lives themselves. That kind of situation doesn't work either.

The truth is, too many Christian parents have not trained their children in the way they should go. They have allowed the public schools and their children's peers to train them in worldly ways instead.

And raising children isn't going to get any easier. The problems in this day and age will only become greater and manifest even more quickly as time goes on. Parents have only one hope of raising godly seed on this earth: They must make the Word of God their standard for training up their children.

Now, a lot of people don't want to hear that. Many parents don't want to be told what they should or should not do in raising their children. Their attitude is, "My home is my castle, and it's no one else's business what happens there."

Well, I just have one question. Does anyone in your home know Jesus? Because if even one person in your home has made Jesus the Lord or "controller" of his or her life — whether it's a mom or a dad or a grandma or a daughter or a son — then it's Jesus' business what goes on there.

Hook Up to God's Word

So in the area of disciplining our children, we have to hook up to what God's Word says, not what the flesh says, not what psychiatry says, not what modern society says. "But this is the '90s, Brother

Sturgeon." It doesn't make any difference what year it is. The Word works regardless of the date on the calendar!

When I teach on godly discipline, people tell me, "Well, Brother Sturgeon, you're old-fashioned." If that's true, then *God* is old-fashioned! But God is eternal Life; there isn't anything old about Him.

God knew what it would be like in our day. He knows what it will be like in the days ahead of us. He knows everything about us, our beginning and our end. That's the kind of God we serve.

So it is foolish for us to say we can't use His way of discipline because it's old-fashioned. God always was, He always is, and He always will be. His Word never changes. And as we search the Scriptures on discipline, we can find the answer to every problem and every situation that comes our way.

If we as Christian parents will do what the Word says in raising our children, the Word will lift up a standard against the devil when he tries to harm them. There will be times that the Spirit of the Lord will arrest us and say, "Pray for your child," and we won't find any peace until we do what the Holy Spirit is telling us to do.

You need to yield to those inner promptings when they come. I know from experience how important it is to be sensitive to the Holy Spirit and to obey the Word in raising children.

It has taken many years for Dea and me to reach the level of spiritual maturity we have in our marriage and as parents. But I'll tell you what — we aren't going back to where we once were! We will just continue to go from glory to glory. I will do my best, Dea will do her best, and all of our children will do their best to grow up into the stature of the fullness of Christ.

God — The Final Authority

You see, from God's perspective, a family is a *spiritual* union. Therefore, He has ordained a divine order of authority in the home. If God isn't made the final authority in the home, then every person will assume his or her own authority. Family members will all do what is right in their own eyes. There will be no order, no consistent standard for each family member to follow.

Now, you may be one of those who thinks that when teenagers reach a certain age, they ought to be able to assume their own authority and make up their own mind on important matters. Well, let me ask you a question: How wise were *you* at that age?

I don't know how many times I said to my boys when they were teenagers, "I'm older than you are. I know where you're headed. Now, you may be right in this particular situation. If you are, God will tell me. If I'm wrong, I'll apologize. But until God tells me, we're going to do it my way. This is just the way it's going to be."

You see, you can be a disciplinarian and still be a lover. You can be a disciplinarian and not be domineering. Men, I'm especially talking to you!

Disciplining God's Way

God and His Word need to be Lord over the home. His way of discipline works. Second Samuel 22:31 says, **As for God, His way is perfect.** You can't improve on what God says to do.

God has given the parents the responsibility of training the children— spirit, soul and body. So if parents want peace in their home, they ought to discipline their children the way God tells them to do it. A *child needs parents who will read God's Word and obey it in every area of life* — particularly in child discipline.

You see, children don't just automatically grow up into mature adults. There is more to rearing children than just giving them a place to stay. Children become what they learn from experiences in the home. Their characters — their personality strengths and weaknesses, their attitudes and values — are in large part formed by Mom and Dad.

Children are like plants. A plant that isn't properly watered, nourished, pruned or given proper sunlight may grow, but it will be disfigured. It won't become what God created it to be. Likewise, children who lack a balance of parental love, guidance and discipline won't become the godly adults God intends for them to be.

God wants us to *do His Word always* in every area of life. According to the Word, that's the only way we will establish godly, successful homes on this earth.

> **O that there were such an heart in them, that they would fear me, and keep all my commandments always, that it might be well with them, and with their children for ever!**
>
> **Deuteronomy 5:29**
>
> **Observe and hear all these words which I command thee, that it may go well with thee, and with thy children after thee for ever, when thou doest that which is good and right in the sight of the Lord thy God.**
>
> **Deuteronomy 12:28**
>
> **I have been young, and now am old; yet have I not seen the righteous forsaken, nor his seed begging bread. He is ever merciful, and lendeth; and his seed is blessed.**
>
> **Psalm 37:25-26**

God says that fools want to do things their own way: **The fear of the Lord is the beginning of knowledge: but fools despise wisdom and instruction** (Prov. 1:7). Fools think they know better than God does. But wise parents will establish their home according to God's Word, because **as for God, his way is perfect; the word of the Lord is tried: he is a buckler to all of them that trust in him** (2 Sam. 22:31).

The Responsibility of the Father in Discipline

So let's see what God says in His Word about child discipline. For one thing, the Bible tells us that God approves of us when we discipline our children according to the Word.

In Genesis 18:19, God said the thing He liked about Abraham was that he would make his children do what they were supposed to do:

For I know him, that he will command his children and his household after him, and they shall keep the way of the Lord, to do justice and judgment; that the Lord may bring upon Abraham that which He hath spoken of him.

God spoke blessings upon Abraham. He knew Abraham would receive these blessings as a result of keeping his household in divine order, which included having obedient children. God knew that Abraham was a man who would raise his children to know how to walk in the ways of the Lord. God knew He could trust Abraham to discipline his children.

Proverbs 4:1 says, **Hear, ye children, the instruction of a father, and attend to know understanding.** This doesn't mean that mothers don't have a part in the discipline of their children. But I truly believe that God desires the father to be the principal parent to administer discipline to a child.

Of course, when children are small, it's a different situation. At six o'clock in the evening when father comes home from work, young children don't remember that they did something wrong at nine o'clock in the morning. So the mother should administer discipline to her small children immediately after the offense so that they know exactly what they are being disciplined for.

Even when children are older, parents have to use wisdom in this area of child discipline. The father should discipline the children when he is present at home. But if he isn't there when a child does something deserving of discipline, it may not be wise to wait for him to come home. That is almost a punishment in itself! And I will tell you what is likely to happen: The devil will tempt the child to start praying and believing God that Daddy won't come home, because when Daddy arrives, Junior will get a spanking!

For example, one time a pastor's teenage son came to me privately after I taught on this subject, and he told me, "You know, Mama would always say, 'Just wait until your dad comes home. I'm going to tell him what you did.' Well, I knew when Dad got home, he would give me a spanking. So even though I knew better, one night I prayed, 'Lord, let Dad have a car wreck so he won't come home. Do whatever it takes to keep him away!'"

This pastor's son hadn't really wanted God to cause his father to have a car wreck. But after the boy heard me minister the Word on this subject, he saw his error and repented for ever even praying that way.

What Is Discipline?

The word *discipline* comes from the root word *disciple.* A disciple is a pupil. Jesus told us to go and *teach* all nations to observe God's commands (Matt. 28:19-20). This command includes our children.

We may have a burning desire to disciple the world for Jesus, but God tells us where to start:

> **But ye shall receive power, after that the Holy Ghost is come upon you: and ye shall be witnesses unto me both *in Jerusalem*, and in all Judaea, and in Samaria, and unto the uttermost part of the earth.**
>
> **Acts 1:8**

God instructed the disciples to begin ministering God's Word in Jerusalem where they were. Only then they were to spread the gospel to the rest of the world. Likewise, we must begin our ministry in our homes to *our own children* before we reach out to the world — or even to the next town!

Love Chastens

The relationship of an earthly father to his children should reflect the relationship of God our Father to us, His children.

> For WHOM THE LORD LOVETH HE CHASTENETH, **and scourgeth every son whom he receiveth. If ye endure chastening, God dealeth with you as with sons; for** WHAT SON IS HE WHOM THE FATHER CHASTENETH NOT? **But if ye be without chastisement, whereof all are partakers, then are ye bastards, and not sons.**
>
> **Furthermore we have had fathers of our flesh which corrected us, and we gave them reverence: shall we not much rather be in subjection unto the Father of spirits, and live? For they verily for a few days chastened us after their own pleasure; but he for our profit that we might be partakers of his holiness.**
>
> **Now no chastening for the present seemeth to be joyous, but grievous: nevertheless afterward it yieldeth the peaceable fruit of righteousness unto them which are exercised thereby.**
>
> **Hebrews 12:6-11**

Now let's apply the above Scripture to our family situations. The Bible says that love chastens. Therefore, parents who love their children should chasten them. We see that God expects us to discipline our children. When we diligently discipline them, they will yield the peaceable fruit of righteousness in their lives.

Let me add that all people are partakers of chastisement in one way or another. A person who seeks God and walks in the light he has received is chastened by a God of love. When that person misses it and realizes he has done something contrary to God's Word, his spirit becomes grieved, and he hastens to repent so he can be pleasing to God once more.

The important thing to remember is that God is a God of love and chastens in love. He is the Father of spirits and chastens in the Spirit.

A person who is walking in Satan's territory will be open to the devices of the devil — poverty, sickness and death. These devices are *not* a form of God's loving chastisement. Jesus stated that **the thief** [the devil] **cometh not, but for to steal, and to kill, and to destroy: I am come that they might have life, and that they might have it more abundantly** (John 10:10).

Remember: God is the giver of all good gifts (James 1:17). So don't allow the devil to rob you through sickness, disease or disastrous circumstances and then blame it on "God's chastening." No! *God chastens in the Spirit and in love.*

God Has Given You What You Need

Many parents feel they lack the power to discipline their children. This is not true. Remember that in Acts 1:8, Jesus promised that *all* power would be given to believers through the infilling of the Holy Spirit.

If you are born again, the Greater One dwells within you (1 John 4:4). And when you receive the baptism of the Holy Spirit, you receive all the power and ability you could ever need for any challenge in life, including the disciplining of your children.

Of course, it is still your God-given responsibility to *assume* the authority in your home. Then you must trust God to supply the power to operate in that authority in the Spirit and in love.

You may not feel wise enough to deal with your children. But God will be faithful to guide you in training them. As you determine to obey the Word, ask Him how to handle situations, and He will show you. That is His promise to you:

> **I will instruct thee and teach thee in the way which thou shalt go: I will guide thee with mine eye. Be ye not as the horse, or as the mule, which have no understanding: whose mouth must be held in with bit and bridle, lest they come near unto thee.**
>
> **Psalm 32:8-9**

God will never leave you nor forsake you. He is able and willing to help you raise godly children, no matter what circumstances may arise in your life.

Discipline Now

Don't delay in making the decision to discipline your children according to God's Word. Children who are not disciplined in their youth suffer for it later in life. The Bible says, **It is good for a man that he bear the yoke [of divine disciplinary dealings] in his youth** (Lam. 3:27, AMP).

Most young people in prisons are there because they finally ran into someone with more authority than themselves. Everyone is going to have to submit to authority sometime in life. The sooner a child learns to submit to authority, the easier it will be for him to live with it.

So if you haven't been training your children as the Word teaches, confess it as sin according to 1 John 1:9. Then make a strong, quality decision to train them as the Word instructs. Determine to consistently administer discipline and love to your children.

Don't Just Teach — Train

God wants us to *train* our children: **Train up a child in the way he should go: and when he is old, he will not depart from it**

(Prov. 22:6). There is much more to training a child than just teaching them godly principles.

According to *Webster's Dictionary*, *to train* means "to mold the character; to instruct by exercise; drill; to make obedient to orders; to prepare for a contest; *to point in an exact direction.*" [1]

How do you point your children in the right direction? You make them obedient to your orders, which are to be in line with God's Word. You mold their character — not after your character, but after the character of the Father God. You are still working on your character; it still has flaws. But God's character is perfect.

However, you can't mold your children's character after the character of God unless you spend time with Him. God has invited you to come up into the heavenlies to spend time with Him. You can go before His throne with boldness to find help in time of need (Heb. 4:16).

Many parents don't know which direction to point their children because they don't know which way to go themselves. Parents who aren't at rest with God cannot train their children correctly.

A father and mother must be able to flow in the wisdom of God. Parents have to know in their hearts that they are going the right direction as they control and direct their children's lives.

What Training Is *Not*

Training is not just teaching a child principles and then letting him decide whether or not to use them. A surprised mother learned that lesson one day after I had ministered on child discipline.

Her teenage daughter broke into tears in front of her and said, "Mom, why do you think I've done the wrong things I have done?" the

---

[1] *Webster's New Collegiate Dictionary* (Cambridge, MA: Riverside, 1961), p. 901.

girl cried. "Because you let me do anything I wanted to. I've always wanted you to tell me what I could and couldn't do."

Some parents teach but don't train their children. For example, suppose a parent threatens a child over and over, "I told you that I'd spank you if you don't take out the garbage" until he finally raises his voice in anger. That parent hasn't trained his child to obey. He has taught the child *not to obey until his parents get angry and yell!*

That's the way some parents handle every discipline situation. When their child does something wrong, they yell and scream, "Why did you do such a thing?" That's not training; that's just telling the child that everything is all right until the old man starts screaming. At that point, he *may* need to listen to what Dad has to say.

Children's Training Applied to Life

Training a child is different. God wants us to train our children how to best use what we have taught them — how to apply it to their lives.

For example, when your child doesn't do what he should, you should warn him once. Then if he disobeys, administer discipline. Train your child to obey you the *first* time you tell him to do something in a normal tone. This trains him later in life to obey the Holy Spirit at His first prompting.

So often when asked to do something, our children stomp out of the room, slamming the door behind them on their way to doing it. It is our responsibility as parents to train our children to obey us *quietly* and *promptly.*

What Do We Teach Our Children?

If your children are to be taught anything, they need to be *taught of the Lord*: **And all thy children shall be taught of the Lord; and great shall be the peace of thy children** (Isa. 54:13).

Your children need to know the Scriptures. God's Word should become a familiar reality in their lives as you minister its truth to them in every possible way throughout each day.

> **And thou shalt teach them** [God's words] **diligently unto thy children, and shalt talk of them when thou sittest in thine house, and when thou walkest by the way, and when thou liest down, and when thou risest up.**
>
> **Deuteronomy 6:7**

Now, if it worked under the Old Covenant for parents to diligently teach their children God's Word, why wouldn't it work under the New Covenant? Well, it may not be working very well because Mom and Dad are in the den all the time watching their favorite television programs!

We parents can waste so much time that could be spent in some way teaching God's principles to our children. God told the Old Testament saints to talk about His Law to their children when they were at home sitting down, when they walked together, when they were lying down to rest and when they were rising to start a new day. That just about includes every waking hour!

Teaching the Word To Our Infants and Toddlers

Children can be taught the Word of God from the time they are infants. For instance, I know one church that endeavors to minister to the spirit, soul and body of each baby who is brought to the nursery.

The nursery workers put simple Scriptures and pictures of Jesus with little children on index cards to show the babies. As a baby sits in an infant chair on the table, a worker shows that picture of Jesus and reads the Scripture on the card to the infant over and over for fifteen minutes.

Then after taking about fifteen minutes to minister to the baby's physical needs, the workers place the infant in a little swing for another fifteen minutes, playing praise and worship tapes for him to listen to. They continue to repeat this process until the church service is over.

It is interesting to observe the children who have gone through this simple process of teaching the Word since they were born. I remember one little four-year-old girl in particular. She was standing next to her grandfather as I talked to him before the afternoon meeting.

We were in the midst of a series of meetings, and the people attending were physically tired. But when this man said to his grand-daughter, "Kara, guess what we're going to do this afternoon? We're going to go to church!" that little girl jumped up and down and clapped her hands with joy!

Of course, that's just the way God showed one church to reach even their youngest children with the gospel. There are many methods to teach God's Word to children.

As the Sturgeon children were growing up, Dea and I kept praise and worship tapes playing in the home throughout the day. We also regularly read the Word to our children. Another thing we found to be very helpful with our children was to play tapes of the Bible or of faith-filled Bible teachings as they went to sleep at night. That way the spoken Word was going forth in their room to minister to their spirits, which never sleep.

It was especially important for the children to hear the Word as they fell asleep when they needed healing in their bodies. For instance, when our son Shane was saved and baptized in the Holy Spirit at age four, the life of God just radiated from him. Several times when he needed healing, Dea and I woke up in the middle of the night to the sound of our son saying over and over in his sleep, "Thank You, Jesus, I'm healed. Thank You, Jesus, I'm healed."

But whatever method you use to feed the Word of God to your children, you can be assured that God's Word will never return void (Isa. 55:11). They *will* be taught of the Lord, and great will be their peace!

Hannah's Faithful Training of Samuel

Let's look to the Word of God to see the difference between *training* and *teaching* children.

> **So Hannah rose up after they had eaten in Shiloh, and after they had drunk. Now Eli the priest sat upon a seat by a post of the temple of the Lord. And she was in bitterness of soul, and prayed unto the Lord, and wept sore.**
>
> **And she vowed a vow, and said, O Lord of hosts, if thou wilt indeed look on the affliction of thine handmaid, and remember me, and not forget thine handmaid, but wilt give unto thine handmaid a man child, then I will give him unto the Lord all the days of his life, and there shall no razor come upon his head.**
>
> **1 Samuel 1:9-11**

Hannah was a woman who walked uprightly before God and desired the blessing of children in her life. She wanted to be fruitful for her husband. When she had endured all the persecution she could endure from her husband's other wife, she came grieving to God.

As Hannah prayed in the temple, she began to make a vow before the Lord. She didn't do this lightly; she fully intended to carry out the vow. God knew she would be faithful.

Notice that Hannah believed for a *man-child*. We see from this account that it is possible to believe for a particular sex of a child yet to be conceived. Hannah believed for a son before conception, and God heard and answered her prayer. In fact, Samuel means "heard of God."

In making a vow to God, Hannah was pronouncing a dedication upon Samuel. You, too, should speak words of dedication over your unborn child.

I know a woman who had ten children, all of whom chose to live ungodly lives. But by the time this mother became pregnant with her eleventh child, she had learned more about the things of God, so this time she prayed a prayer of dedication over her unborn son.

As time passed, this son became the first of the children to be born again and Spirit-filled. And he has been used of God over the years to minister to his other brothers and sisters. He has seen many of them confess Jesus as Lord.

So dedicate your unborn children to serve Jesus as their Lord. If you already have children and you didn't do that, then believe that your children will be saved because they belong to your household (Acts 16:31).

Now let's look at Hannah's faithfulness as a mother to train her son in the ways of the Lord.

> **And when she [Hannah] had weaned him, she took him up with her, with three bullocks, and one ephah of flour, and a bottle of wine, and brought him unto the house of the Lord in Shiloh: and the child was young. And they slew a bullock, and brought the child to Eli.**
>
> **And she said, Oh my lord, as thy soul liveth, my lord, I am the woman that stood by thee here, praying unto the Lord. For this child I prayed; and the Lord hath given me my petition which I asked of him:**
>
> **Therefore also I have lent him to the Lord; as long as he liveth he shall be lent to the Lord. And he worshipped the Lord there.**
>
> **1 Samuel 1:24-28**

Hannah brought Samuel to live in the temple according to her commitment that he would serve God all of his life. From the time Samuel was born, she had trained him to go in that direction. Samuel grew up faithfully serving God, just as Hannah had trained him. As a child, he ever hastened to do Eli's bidding, even in the middle of the night.

As time passed, Samuel became God's man in Israel. The Bible tells us that God didn't let one of Samuel's words ever fall to the ground (1 Sam. 3:19). Samuel never said an inoperable, faithless word.

Improper Training:
The Example of Eli and His Sons

Contrary to Hannah, Eli the priest did *not* control or train his boys in the way they should go. He did a poor job of raising them.

Now the sons of Eli were sons of Belial [the devil]; **they knew not the Lord....**

Now Eli was very old, and heard all that his sons did unto all Israel; and how they lay with the women that assembled at the door of the tabernacle of the congregation. And he said unto them, Why do ye such things? for I hear of your evil dealings by all this people. Nay, my sons; for it is no good report that I hear: ye make the Lord's people to transgress.

1 Samuel 2:12, 22-24

Eli's sons were disobedient and immoral. Notice that Eli used nothing but *words* to discipline his sons. He neglected to train his sons, and, consequently, they neglected to listen to him. *Scolding is not training.*

Eli didn't train his sons to obey him or the Word. (Actually, we need to train our children to obey the Word even more than us, because although we can miss it sometimes, the Word never does.)

Don't Honor Your Children Over God

Look at the accusation the Lord made against Eli regarding his sons:

Wherefore kick ye at my sacrifices and at mine offering, which I have commanded in my habitation; and honourest thy sons above me, to make yourselves fat with the chiefest of all the offerings of Israel my people?
1 Samuel 2:29

Eli's sons were taking more than their proper share of the priests' privileges. And because Eli allowed them to take unfair advantage of their priestly office, God said that Eli was favoring or honoring his sons over Him.

When you allow your children to disobey you, you are honoring them before God and His Word.

If a child is a disobedient child, then the parent is probably a disobedient parent. God expects parents to train their children. If parents neglect to obey God's Word in this area, they are out of the will of God.

Remember, too, that spiritual principles will work negatively as well as positively for you. If you sow poor child discipline, you will reap disobedient children just as Eli did.

Both Hannah and Eli spent their lives serving God. But whereas Hannah was obedient to God in training her children (she had five more after Samuel), Eli disobeyed God by not controlling his sons.

Protected From Ungodly Influence

However, even though Hannah sent her son to live with Eli, the influence of his ungodly sons never affected Samuel. Why? Because Mama and Daddy had already prayed and used their faith, dedicating their son to the Lord.

That's the answer for single parents who ask, "When my child goes to visit my divorced spouse, who is living an ungodly life, how can I expect him to come back unaffected by that ungodly influence?"

Samuel was lent, or dedicated, to the Lord. Therefore, no matter what circumstances he faced living at the temple, they never affected him. In fact, as Samuel grew up, he became the only one who actually heard from God.

The Word says that there was no open vision in Israel under Eli's ministry (1 Sam. 3:1). Eli hadn't had a vision or heard from God in years. His ministry had become increasingly less effective as he continued to miss God concerning his sons.

And Eli's sons sure didn't hear from God because they were lying with prostitutes at the gate of the temple!

(Notice that God expected Eli's sons, who were grown men old enough to have sex with the prostitutes, to be under submission to their father. And God expected Eli to control his grown sons. You ask, "How long am I responsible for my children? How long do they have to obey me?" As long as they live in your house!)

Finally, God completely cut Eli's family out of the priesthood.

> **For I have told him that I will judge his house for ever for the iniquity which he knoweth; because his sons made themselves vile, and he restrained them not.**
>
> **1 Samuel 3:13**

When Eli's sons had strayed too far into Satan's territory and away from God's protection, both the sons and Eli were killed. Not only that, but all Israel was affected by this family's disobedience because the sons lost the Ark of the Covenant to the enemy before their deaths (1 Sam. 3:13).

This account of Eli and his sons shows us that neglecting to train our children can have disastrous results — not only for us and our children, but for the body of Christ.

Obedient for Generations

Besides Samuel, the Word gives us other examples of obedient children who reaped God's blessings. For instance, in the book of Jeremiah God talks about the sons of a man named Jonadab:

> **The command which Jonadab the son of Rechab gave to his sons not to drink wine, has been carried out and established [as a custom for more than two hundred years]; to this day they drink no wine, but have obeyed their father's command. But I, even I, have persistently spoken to you, but you have not listened and obeyed Me....**
>
> **And Jeremiah said to the house of the Rechabites, Thus says the Lord of hosts, the God of Israel: Because you have obeyed the commandment of Jonadab your father, and kept all his precepts, and done according to all that he commanded you; Therefore thus says the Lord of hosts, the God of Israel: Jonadab the son of Rechab shall never lack a man [descendant] to stand before Me.**
>
> **Jeremiah 35:14,18-19, AMP**

Two hundred years before Jeremiah's ministry, Jonadab had given his sons a command to drink no wine. For two centuries, his descendants obeyed Jonadab's words. This obedience to parental authority so pleased God that He promised to give Jonadab male descendants forever.

Setting Your House in Order

You may ask, "What if my children are older and I didn't train them according to the Word when they were young?" Well, if it took you years to get into the mess you're in with your children, it may be difficult at first as you start training and disciplining them God's way. You have to expect that the devil will do everything he possibly can to keep you from setting your house in God's order so you can have peace in your home.

But I will tell you this: When the time is limited and your commitment to obey God in this area is strong, God has a way of taking hold of a home situation with authority and power so that things happen very quickly to set the home in order!

Now that we have seen the importance of administering effective, godly discipline in our homes, these questions arise next: "How do I train my children?" and "What does God's Word say about training children?"

Two main elements are found in the Bible for the effective training of children: *love* and *control*. You can't control a child that you don't love, and you can't love a child you don't control. In the next two chapters, we will explore these two vital elements.

How To Love Your Children

The love walk is of primary importance to us as Christians because we are children of a loving God. The Word tells us that God *is* love (1 John 4:8). In everything we do, we are to follow His example of love.

Be ye therefore followers of God as dear children: And walk in love, as Christ also hath loved us, and hath given himself for us an offering and a sacrifice to God for a sweetsmelling savour.

Ephesians 5:1-2

We must extend the same agape love to our children that we show toward our brethren. In fact, our love walk must *begin* in the home.

God has placed you as the head of your home not only to discipline, but also to minister love to your children — the agape kind of love that ministers to another person's need without thought of personal gain.

God ministers His love to us through His Word. In the same way, you should spend time in the Word with your children. Teach them spiritual truths. Teach them their rights as sons of God and their authority in Christ Jesus. Let them know that they aren't fighting flesh and blood, but principalities and powers (Eph. 6:12).

Develop Mutual Trust

Develop a relationship of mutual trust with your children so you can say about them what God said about Abraham: **For I know him**

(Gen. 18:19). Let your children know that you trust them. Give them reason to trust you. Your children should be assured that you are walking close to God so they will be free to seek your counsel.

Be honest and humble with your children when you miss it as a parent. Admit your mistakes and ask their forgiveness.

To be an effective leader in your home, you must establish this type of relationship with your children. You will find that they easily accept a relationship with you based on mutual trust and respect. They will begin to voluntarily come to you to seek your forgiveness about minor transgressions that don't even merit discipline.

Also, in order to develop a good relationship with your children, you have to take time with them. When you want them to do something that is new to them, show them exactly how to perform the task. Don't have an older brother or sister show them. Let each child know that he is equally important to you and worth your time. Remember, one of the definitions of *to train* is "to instruct by exercise."

Finally, make sure you leave your job at the job. The time you spend with your children should be spent enjoying activities of mutual interest.

Treat Your Children as Little People

Treat your children as little people, not inferior beings. They are just as capable of getting saved and filled with the Holy Spirit as an adult is — maybe even more so!

For example, I mentioned that our youngest son, Shane, was four years old when he was saved and filled with the Holy Spirit. At that time, our two older boys had already been saved and Spirit-filled.

Our children's salvation was not difficult because ever since they were very young, they had known nothing but the Word of faith in our home. Also, at bedtime Dea would kneel and pray with the boys. And each night until they were born again, she would ask each one, "Son, would you like to receive Jesus as your Lord and Savior?"

The night Shane said "yes" to that question, Dea prayed earnestly with him. Then she asked, "Now that you know Jesus, do you want to receive the baptism of the Holy Spirit?" Every night she approached Shane with that question until finally one night, Shane said "yes," and something happened.

That night Dea prayed as usual with the boys at bedtime, including a prayer for Shane to be filled with the Holy Spirit. Then as Shane climbed into bed, Dea noticed he had dirty feet. She told him, "You can't go to bed with dirty feet like that!"

Dea marched Shane into the bathroom, set him up on the counter and put his feet in warm water. Then as Dea washed Shane's feet, all of a sudden he started speaking in tongues! He began to pray in the Spirit with such fervency that he just fell over into Dea's arms, laughing and praying in tongues with his feet still in the warm water!

At that same moment, I was walking down the hallway, and I heard my little son praying in the Spirit. I froze, then I turned around and walked back to the bathroom. I stared at Shane.

"He's speaking in tongues!" I exclaimed incredulously.

Dea laughed and said, "Yes, he is!"

The next day, the entire family was in our car, heading for a meeting where I was to be the speaker. An older lady from the church was traveling with us. Shane was standing on the hump of the backseat floorboard (this was before the days of seat belts!), watching the road ahead of us.

Suddenly I had an idea. "Why don't we all pray in tongues for a while?" I asked. "Shane, do you want to pray in tongues?"

"Uh, huh," Shane nodded.

So we all began to pray in the Spirit. Shane started to pray the same way he had the night before — but this time he fell right over into this lady's arms, laughing and praying in the Holy Ghost!

So treat your children as little people. Don't talk down to them. Look into their eyes, and have them look straight into your eyes when you are conversing with them. This is especially important when you are disciplining them, but you should always make a practice of maintaining eye contact with your children. A child's self-image is not improved by a father or mother who talks to him behind a newspaper.

Speak Faith Over Your Children

An important part of loving your children is to speak your faith over them. Confess to them what the Word says about them. Tell them who they are in Christ Jesus.

As your children grow older, continue to maintain your confession. See your children as proper children, just as Moses' parents saw him (Heb. 11:23). Don't even imagine your children out in the world getting into trouble. In spite of any situations that may arise to contradict your stance of faith, hold fast to your confession that your children are proper children.

I have a friend whose daughter left home to pursue the evil lifestyle that the world offers. The father told his daughter that she was a proper child and therefore would not enjoy drinking or taking drugs. He maintained his confession in spite of the apparent circumstances to the contrary.

Finally, one day this man's daughter told him she wasn't having any fun drinking or taking drugs and asked if she could come home. The father replied, "I had never considered you gone, because you are a proper child!"

You see, as you speak the Word over your children, you are building a spiritual hedge of protection around them. You are saying those things that are not as though they were, and your children will eventually become what you are speaking in faith! (Rom. 4:17).

For instance, if your children are out in the world taking a wrong path in life, you should confess, "Father, my babies are coming home. I thank You that they are disciples taught of the Lord, obedient to God's Word. Great is their peace and undisturbed composure (Isa. 54:13, AMP).

"My children are the head and not the tail. They're above and not beneath (Deut. 28:13). They are more than conquerors in Christ Jesus (Rom. 8:37). And they desire to seek the prize of the high calling of God in Christ Jesus! (Phil. 3:14)."

As you speak what God says about your absent children, He goes to work to bring that Word to pass in their lives. Remember, the arm of the Lord isn't shortened by distance. In fact, there *is* no distance in the spirit realm.

Many parents don't understand the untold damage they cause in their children's lives by the negative words they speak about them. Some parents say, "That child is going to be the death of me." Or they will laugh and say, "That child has given me every gray hair I have!" You can see how the devil tries to find an open door into a family through such words — even to the point of causing death.

Rejected From the Womb

Some children were rejected with negative words from the time of conception onward. For instance, when a married couple finds out that the wife is pregnant, they may decide, "We don't need another child; we should abort this one." Or the husband may say to people, "My wife is pregnant — but we need another kid like we need a hole in the head!" That child is being rejected by his parents' words while still in the womb.

These parents are actually speaking into the spirit of their unborn child, saying, "We don't want you," and the baby's spiritual ears can pick up on what they are saying. Then if the parents go ahead and have that unwanted child, they wonder why they have more trouble with him or her than they did with their other children!

Your words have great power in the spirit realm. That truth can work both positively and negatively in your life.

For example, even though my father was a Christian and loved God, he often said, "I'll die a young man" — and he did.

Dad underwent open-heart surgery in Oklahoma City back in 1967. As he lay in the hospital room recuperating, a lady from the community whose husband had undergone the same operation kept telling my mother, "Pearl, don't get your hopes up until after the seventeenth day. You know that my husband died on the seventeenth day. Don't get your hopes until after the seventeenth day."

We heard those words from that woman day in and day out. And on what day did my dad die? The seventeenth day after the surgery.

I am telling you, you will have what you say. So stop talking ornery words about your spouse. Stop telling your children, "You'll never change." Begin to let the Lord build your house by saying what He says about your family (Ps. 127:1).

Confess and pray the Word over your children. Say faith-filled things about them that they haven't even seen about themselves. Treat them as if they were already saved, filled with the Holy Ghost and serving God. Before long, they will start acting like the words you have been speaking over them.

A Mother's Steadfast Confession of Faith

Not too many Christians who call themselves "faith people" are steadfast in their confession of faith over their children. They often learn how to speak faith in other areas of their lives — but when it comes to their own children, they speak what they see. For instance, when their child does something wrong, instead of dealing with the offense in love and faith, parents often browbeat their child, yelling at him, "*What did you do that for?*"

The testimony of a woman minister friend of mine regarding her son demonstrates the power of confessing God's Word over your children. This minister is a strong woman of God who years ago put together a confession of faith, based entirely on the Word, to speak over one's children.

Later, this woman's son got involved with drugs. Bad news travels fast, and as she traveled in the ministry, people would ask her, "What about your son? How is he doing?"

But this mother stayed strong in faith. Every time someone asked about her son, she would answer, "Oh, he's a disciple taught of the Lord, obedient to God's Word, and great is his peace and undisturbed composure." That was even her answer the day after her son stole all of her fur coats and sold them for drugs!

For years this woman and her husband maintained their confession of faith about their son. The mother would even go up to people and say, "I just want to tell you about my son." When they asked, "Well, what about him?" she would reply, "He is a disciple taught of the Lord, obedient to God's Word, and great is his peace and undisturbed composure."

Then one night in New York at one of David Wilkerson's Teen Challenge meetings, this son was born again and filled with the Holy Spirit. Today he is an on-fire preacher, ministering the gospel of the Lord Jesus Christ!

But back when the situation with this young man looked hopeless, his parents would not waver from speaking what the Word of God said about him rather than what they saw. This woman and her husband knew their son had the Word in his heart, and they weren't going to allow the devil to steal his life. So they continually spoke their faith over him until he became what they were speaking.

Demonstrate Your Love

Your actions of love are as important as your words of love to your children. You need to *show* them that you love them.

Don't wait for a special occasion to show affection. Don't hug your children only after disciplining them or after they have done something special to please you. Instead, take opportunities to hug and kiss your children just because you love them. Otherwise, you teach them that they must earn your love by performing a certain way.

Most people who have trouble believing that God loves them have had unloving earthly fathers. This is why it is so extremely important for a father to be quick to give his children physical assurances of his love. There is nothing unmanly about a father hugging and kissing his sons.

Always maintain an attitude of love with your children. Continually try to find things about which you can compliment them.

Many children have grown up as disappointments to their parents because through the years, the parents continually emphasized their child's weak points.

Don't make that mistake. Instead of always pointing out your child's faults to him, point out his good traits. Tell him that you have faith in him to do better in his weak points. *Remember that your words have power.* Your children will become what you say about them. And they have a way of fulfilling your expectations of them!

It is largely the parents who form the child's character. For example, before I was saved, my wife and I raised our first son Mike very strictly, demanding top performance of him. When our second son

Brian came along, we expected him to do the same things our first son was doing, although Mike was several years older.

I would tell Brian to do something, and when he fumbled around unsuccessfully, I'd irritably say, "Sit down, Brian; you can't do it right anyway. Mike, you do it."

For instance, Mike took to bike riding with ease, but Brian had problems from the start, mainly because I expected him to be clumsy and fall.

Brian never could ride well until after I made Jesus Lord of my life and began to make positive confessions about him. In fact, by the time I was saved, Brian had developed a very poor self-image in general because of our *words* and our *attitudes* toward him.

Then as God taught us differently, Brian began to develop into a self-confident person. One day the school held a bike contest, and it seemed that Brian was the worst bicyclist in the crowd. But I looked in his eyes and said, "Go win in the name of Jesus!" Brian took his place in the contest, knowing that his dad believed in him — and he came home with first place honors!

So be a *stimulator*, not a *reactor*. Stop reacting to your child's faults. Look for opportunities to build good traits in him.

Sometimes the devil will tempt a child to misuse one of his positive traits in a negative way. For example, your child may be noisy (negative), but you can show him that he is a very *alert* (positive) child. He could be prone to have "*pity parties*" (negative), but that is *compassion* misused. A child who is *aggressively overconfident* (negative) needs to be shown how to walk in *godly confidence* (positive).

The list of negative traits and their positive counterparts can go on and on. But no matter what your child's qualities and personality traits are, it will take the Word and the Holy Spirit to show you, the parent, how to minister *God's* perspective of those qualities to him or her.

Be an Example

It is important that you set a godly example in front of your children. Don't tell your child to do something you won't do yourself.

Too often the faults of a child reflect those of the parent. In fact, do you know what the problem is with a lot of children? They have seen their parents do the things that they have been told not to do!

For example, my daddy smoked, and when I was a little boy, I always thought it was cool to pick up a stick and act like I was smoking. Then one day I thought, *Why waste time doing this? Why not just light up a real cigarette?* But when I did just that, I got in big trouble. I couldn't figure out why I got a paddling for something my daddy did!

Also, why should a child have to clean up his bedroom if his parent's bedroom is always a mess? Children know how their parents live; they know what their mom and dad are like.

Parents don't have the right to ask their children to do something they don't practice themselves. If their bedroom looks like a tornado went through it, they ought to set the example and clean their own bedroom before they tell their children to clean theirs.

Set an Example of Honesty

Also, if you are having problems with your child telling lies, check yourself out. He may have heard you telling "white lies" as excuses for avoiding commitments or something you didn't want to do. In God's eyes, lies are lies, and He doesn't approve of them at all.

Children who consistently lie usually have parents who lie. Children aren't born that way. They are taught to lie.

Or perhaps Mom and Dad don't lie, but they allow their child to play with children who do. A child who chronically lies is picking it up somewhere.

Parents have to be very careful not to set the wrong example in the area of lying. For example, in the ministry there have been times I didn't want to tell someone *why* I didn't want to go somewhere, so I gave them an excuse. However, excuses can too easily become lies.

I remember one time the telephone rang, and I answered it. It was a woman who wanted me to come over to their Bible study. I told her, "No, we can't come to your Bible study because we are going over to the Semrads' house."

A little later, I looked out my office door and saw my youngest son all dressed up in his coat and hat, waiting for me to walk out of my office.

"Shane, why do you have your coat and hat on?" I asked.

He replied, "I want to go to Dougie's house."

"But we aren't going to Dougie's house," I said.

Shane walked off, but soon he was back in front of my office door — only this time he was crying. I walked over to him and asked, "What are you crying about, Shane?"

"We're not going to Dougie's house," he whimpered.

"That's right, Son. We're not going to Dougie's house."

"But, Daddy, you said we were going to the Semrads, and Dougie is a Semrad!"

You see, I thought I was just giving that woman an excuse when I said we were going to the Semrads' house with no intention of doing so. But the truth was, I lied. My son heard the name Semrad, and he knew his best friend's name was Dougie Semrad. So because he believed his daddy, he got ready to go!

Now, someone may say, "Well, sometimes you just have to bend the truth in order not to offend someone." No, you don't ever have to do that. Isaiah 30:9 says that lying children are **children that will not hear the law of the Lord.**

What do you do instead of lie? You just start telling the truth. In the example I just gave from my own life, if that woman had pressed me to know why I wasn't coming to her Bible study, I should have said, "Because I just really don't want to come." You know, I would rather offend someone who doesn't live in my home by telling the truth than to offend my own children by setting the wrong example and causing them to start lying themselves!

If you are guilty of telling lies, don't whip your child when the school complains that he lies. Clean up your own act first; then be a godly example to him. Likewise, if you see your child stealing, hating, ridiculing and so forth, check yourself out before you lambast him. You may have to confess your own faults first and ask your child to forgive you for being a poor example.

Hear From God for Yourself

We have talked about loving your children enough to speak faith-filled words over them and to set a good example before them. But take heart: You don't have to figure out how to do all this on your own.

Just follow your spirit. Stay open to hear from God in dealing with your children. He has the solution for every problem.

For example, one woman had a son who was reaching the "girl-noticing" age. She sought God for wisdom in dealing with him. The Lord told her to buy her son a cat.

That seemed strange to her at first, but the Lord revealed to her that her son needed an outlet to express love. God wanted him to love and pet the cat instead of the girls.

Because this mother stayed open to God's voice, she found an effective way to meet her son's need before a problem developed. (By the way, don't you immediately go out and buy a cat for your child! This was just the way the Lord ministered to this particular woman.)

Or you may be asking yourself, "How do I deal with my rebellious teenager?" The best thing you can do is to be a man or a woman of prayer. Stay "prayed up" so that when you are around your teenage child, you will be able to speak what Jesus would have you speak.

Don't sit around and plan, "Okay, this is what I'm going to say, and this is what I'm going to do." Just pray in the Spirit about the situation. As you pray, the Lord may give you a vision in which you see what you're supposed to do or say to your teenager. Or you may just come to a place in prayer where you know in your heart what you need to do.

You may not know the exact words you are supposed to say. But when the time comes, the right words will just flow from your heart, because you prayed it out beforehand and heard from God for yourself. You tapped into the heart of the Father.

You may not even think you are saying anything of significance to your child, but the love of God behind your words is powerful enough to break every yoke and to destroy every bondage. What you say and what your child hears may even be two different things, but God will use your Spirit-led words to turn the situation around.

We are about to look at the importance of controlling your children. But you can't control your children if you don't love them. So develop a relationship of mutual respect and trust with your children. Set a godly example before them, and always speak words of faith about them. As you do, you will make the task of training them to be obedient children infinitely easier!

HOW TO CONTROL YOUR CHILDREN

Parents can't *train* a child if they can't *control* him. In many homes, two-year-olds run the entire household. If the two-year-old doesn't want to go where the family planned to go, the whole family stays home. If the two-year-old steals toys from the neighbors, the parents lie to cover up for their little terror. When the two-year-old is caught hitting other children with a piece of pipe, the parents accuse the children of provoking their sweet little baby.

An element of control does exist within a family like this, but it is the wrong kind — everyone is controlled by the two-year-old! This type of situation ought not to be.

Establish Godly Control in Your Home

If you are going to raise godly children, you will have to establish a godly measure of control in your home. In my home, I guarantee you that even my pets know when I say, "No"!

For instance, I used to have a cocker spaniel named Shama Black-bear. *Shama* in the Hebrew language means "obedient one" — and Shama Blackbear *was* obedient!

Cocker spaniels are known to be a little snippy and hyperactive, but not Shama Blackbear. Even when he was a puppy, he knew he had to be Shama, the obedient one.

When we sent Shama to the groomer the first time, the man asked me, "How many times has your dog been groomed before?"

"None," I replied.

"Well," he said, "we'll have to charge you extra because your dog is a cocker. An extra person will be needed to watch him and make sure he doesn't try to bite me as I groom him."

I said, "Just set him on the grooming table and tell him to stand, and he'll stand there." Then I walked out the door, praying more for the groomer's peace of mind than for my dog!

When I arrived home, I received a call from the groomer. The devil said to my mind, "Shama bit him. You're going to get sued." But the groomer said, "This is unbelievable! Your dog just stands there!"

I replied, "Yes, and if you want him to sit, just tell him to sit."

"I've never groomed a dog like this one before," the groomer said.

"Well, we're Christians," I explained. "The dog's name is Shama, which means 'obedient one.' We speak that name over him all the time, and he lives up to it!"

That groomer trimmed Shama for years, and every time he thought, Well, when he grows older, he'll become snippy and bitey. But Shama stayed a good, obedient dog to the end of his life.

Also, I remember how we used to round up cattle on the ranch. The whole family, Dad, Mom, Marcia, Barbara and myself would be needed, and hired hands as well. It would take us two days to round up the cattle out of three pastures. But after I was born again and filled with the Holy Spirit, on roundup day I just rode my horse out to the cattle and told them to go to the corral!

That may sound farfetched, but I'm not kidding. I had two other Spirit-filled Christians riding with me that day, and they thought I was crazy. But two hundred cows and calves and five registered bulls walked right into the corral without a hitch. We didn't have to beat them or holler at them; we didn't have to scream or yell or rope them or drag them in. I just went out to the pasture and told those cattle, "Go to the corral!"

You see, as believers, we have dominion over everything that creeps or crawls on the earth (Gen. 1:28). And if we can exercise our rightful dominion over animals, why shouldn't we be able to do it with our children?

God's Instrument of Control for Children

Training your child will often have to involve a certain amount of force to bring his or her will under submission to your authority. God has ordained an instrument particularly for you to exercise godly control over your child. He has also provided a strategic and well-padded area on your child's body to receive this instrument. Of course, this divine instrument of love is the *rod*!

He that spareth his rod hateth his son: but he that loveth him chasteneth him betimes.

Proverbs 13:24

If you want to obey God and you love your child, you have no choice — you must use the rod. If you can't make yourself apply the rod, you may as well tell your child that you hate him. That's what God says. And notice that He says, "Chasten him *betimes*." This means you are to chasten your child as often as he needs it.

Spanking Drives Out Foolishness

Proverbs 22:15 tells us what spanking a child accomplishes: **Foolishness is bound in the heart of a child; but the rod of correction shall drive it far from him.**

65

The *New International Version* says it this way: **Folly is *bound up* in the heart of a child, but the rod of discipline will drive it far from him.** Folly is bound fast to the heart of every boy and every girl who has ever been born. And it is the parents' duty to drive that folly, or foolishness, far from their child with the rod of discipline.

I will use my middle son, Brian, as an example of how this works. When we lived in the country, the boys were used to wide open spaces. They could ride their bicycles for miles and never see a car. We might see one car pass our house in a day. So the boys could play in the road with their bikes or wagons with no fear of being hit.

Then we moved to town, and it was altogether a different matter. One day I looked out and saw Brian riding his bicycle out of our driveway, across the street, into the neighbor's driveway and back across the street to our driveway again. I knew that was a foolish thing to do because cars frequently drove by. Brian could be hit by a driver who didn't notice him riding into the street from behind a parked car.

So I warned Brian once, saying, "Son, you can't do that." I walked him through a detailed explanation of why it wasn't safe to ride his bike back and forth across the street.

Brian thought it over. "Well, what about the flag I have on my bike? Won't that help drivers see me?" Brian wanted a good reason for stopping this fun game of riding up and down the driveways as if they were bicycle ramps.

I explained that a flag wasn't enough to make the game safe. I told him, "Now, if you do that again, I'll have to spank you."

One day soon after that, I looked out my office window (my office was and still is in our home), and there Brian was again, riding his bike back and forth across the street.

I walked outside, and the moment Brian saw me, he froze. He knew he was in trouble. He said, "Daddy, I won't do it again."

"I know you won't do it again!" I replied.

In other words, Brian was saying, "We don't want to go through with this spanking routine, do we?" And I was saying, "Oh, yes, we do, Son, because following God's instructions on child discipline is the only thing I know to do."

So Brian and I went in the house, and I gave him a spanking. What did that spanking do? It drove that foolishness *far* from him!

I know that concept doesn't make sense to the natural mind, but when we put our faith in the Word of God, it just works!

The Rod Gives Wisdom

It's important to remember that discipline is something done *for* a child, not *to* a child. It is done for the child's good, not because the parent is fed up with his behavior.

Proverbs 29:15 says, **The rod and reproof give wisdom: but a child left to himself bringeth his mother to shame.** What kind of wisdom does the child receive through godly discipline?

Well, when you spank your child, it will hurt him, causing him to want to avoid similar pain in the future. Then the next time he is tempted to break that rule, he will remember the spanking. If the punishment is administered consistently, he will associate the pain with the offense.

However, spanking a child is never to be physical abuse. Improperly administered discipline will result in an oppressed spirit.

Spanking is in the Word, but it has to be done in love, because God is a God of love. We can rest assured that when we control our children as the God of love has instructed us, the results are going to be exactly what He said they would be — our children will be given wisdom.

Don't Browbeat Your Child

There is also such a thing as verbal and mental abuse. Back when I was growing up, we called it *browbeating*.

Remember Eli's continual, useless scolding of his sons. Don't make the same mistake Eli did by beating your child with words. *Browbeating will never replace bottom beating.*

Children neither respect nor respond positively to verbal or mental abuse. But because faith comes by hearing, your negative words will plant negative faith in your child's heart, causing him to believe he is a failure.

Spanked, Not 'Spocked'

Many parents use other methods in disciplining their children besides spanking. In this era, you hear various psychologists including the famous Dr. Benjamin Spock spouting all kinds of theories. But God's eternal truth is much better than any psychological theory. And God's Word says a child should be spanked, not "Spocked"!

I saw the truth of this statement again and again during the years we ran a Christian school for kindergarten through twelfth grade back in the '70s. We asked parents to sign a form giving us permission to discipline their children the way we would discipline our own according to God's Word — by spanking them.

We also ran a Bible training center for adults, and every morning at eight o'clock, the Christian school students and Bible training center students would come together for a half hour of praise and worship.

We would tell the children, "We want you to participate. When we're all standing and lifting holy hands before the Lord, we want you to lift up your hands in worship too."

But one young boy never participated and behaved in ways that distracted the other children. He had a leader's personality and the other children looked up to him, so we knew we couldn't let him get by with his wrong behavior. Otherwise, sooner or later the other children would follow his bad example.

So one morning when he was being particularly disruptive, I grabbed hold of him and more or less dragged him out of the praise and worship service and into my office. The first thing I had to do was ask him to forgive me for the manner in which I took him out of the service. Then I took time to read a list of Scriptures on child discipline from the Bible (see list on pages 169-182).

You see, the Holy Ghost inspired the Word of God, and He will work on the heart of a child when the Word is spoken over him.

After I finished reading, I asked him, "What do you deserve to receive?"

He replied, "I deserve a spanking." I then gave him the spanking we both agreed he deserved.

After his spanking that day, he grew in faith and obedience and became one of our most cooperative students that school year. At the year-end banquet, his father proudly testified that when he told his son to do a task, he knew it would be done without even checking to make sure.

And the week after school ended, Joey still kept showing up at school every day! He stayed at school that entire week while the teachers cleaned up their classrooms for the summer, and he didn't leave until we locked the doors to go home. He loved school that much!

Applying the Rod
Brings Forgiveness and Freedom

When our sons were young and the family was driving on the road at night, I would sometimes have to tell the boys that they would receive a spanking when we arrived home. But sometimes I would forget what I had told them.

Because the boys knew it was God's will for me to discipline them, they would remind me of what I had said, and then we would take care of the situation God's way. You see, my children wanted to live free of condemnation. They realized that the time of correction would be a time of *forgiveness* and *freedom*.

Spanking your child in a scriptural manner clears his conscience of guilt when the enemy comes to condemn him. Once he has asked God and you to forgive him, he will be able to look back to the time of correction and know that he has been forgiven for the offense and that he is free of condemnation.

Guidelines on Administering Discipline

So how *do* you spank your child in a scriptural manner? Well, first of all, you should never use your hand to spank him. Instead, employ a paddle that your child will learn to associate with training. The paddle should have a wide surface (for example, a Ping-Pong paddle), especially if the child is young.

Don't let your children play with the paddle or use it to spank their dolls. The paddle or rod of discipline isn't a toy; it is an instrument of love that should be put up out of the way when it isn't being used to discipline.

Our hands should only be used to affectionately pat or hug our children. God uses His hand to lovingly welcome us into His presence, not to hit us. What a surprise we would have if we came into His presence expecting Him to hug us, and He slapped us instead! If God were to treat us that way, He could slap us clear into an eternity where we would rather not be!

But the Father God never does that. The moment you ask Him for His attention, you are in the throne room with Him. You can go into that throne room with boldness to find mercy and grace to help in time of need.

If parents discipline their child with their hand, he won't know whether they are about to hug him or hit him. It is easy to detect a child who has been spanked with the hand. When the parents raise their hand or reach out to their child, he often flinches or ducks.

If you have ever made a practice of slapping your child with your hand, just determine to stop that method of discipline right now. Ask God and your children to forgive you. Let your hands be associated only with affection and love in your children's minds.

Also, never hit your child on the head. Remember, God has provided a well-padded area on the child's body to receive discipline.

Some people ask, "Do you spank a bare bottom?" No, I don't think that is necessary. In fact, it is probably not advisable, given today's laws defining child abuse. God said that we are to obey the authorities over us. Of course, when the law of the land directly violates God's Word, we will have to obey the Word.

But I don't believe you have to spank your child's bare bottom in order to be effective in discipline. You aren't trying leave marks on him. You should *never* bruise or break your child's skin or discipline him in anger.

Spanking Ministers to a Child's Spirit, Soul and Body

God makes a profound statement about child discipline in Proverbs 23:13-14:

> **Withhold not correction from the child: for if thou beatest [spank] him with the rod, he shall not die. Thou shalt beat him with the rod, and *shalt deliver his soul from hell.***

Why does spanking deliver your child's soul from hell? Because there is a spiritual impartation that takes place when you spank your child. Spanking ministers to the whole person, not just to the child's body. You see, man is a spirit; he has a soul (mind, will and emotions); and he lives in a body.

Your child is a spirit. In training him, you should minister to his spirit. Remember that the spirit is ageless, so you can minister in depth.

I remember one couple who had six children and worked hard to absorb everything I could teach them on godly discipline. But later they said to me, "No matter how consistently we spank our son Brian, nothing seems to work."

I asked them, "Is he born again?"

"Well," they replied, "we don't really know."

"Then spend more time praying with him," I advised. "Be just as consistent as you have been with your discipline, but also be consistent every night to pray with him to receive Jesus and the baptism of the Holy Spirit. Then let's see what happens."

So the couple followed my advice. It wasn't long before he was born again, and his behavior changed overnight.

So if God's way of disciplining your child doesn't seem to be working, make sure he is born again. Secondly, consistently pray with him until he receives the baptism of the Holy Spirit.

Besides praying with your child, getting the Word into his spirit is of primary importance. Only God's Word brings lasting change. Only God's Word will not return void when it is planted in your child's heart. Once the Word is planted, a child's spirit will reveal spiritual truth to his mind.

In our Christian school, we had our students listen to some of the guest speakers who came to speak to our adult training center. Our children would sit for more than an hour and receive the teaching of the Word. Visiting ministers were always impressed with their attentiveness.

We had trained those children to take notes on what they understood. It continually amazed us to read their summaries of the sermons. They were catching hold of the truths in God's Word.

When parents train a child according to the Word, they encourage him to submit his selfish will to authority. A person who is ruled by his selfish will won't make Jesus his Lord. However, a person who knows how to submit to earthly authority won't find it that difficult to accept the Lordship of Jesus in his life. Therefore, the child who knows his parents love him and has been trained to obey their authority will find it easy to allow a loving God to control his life.

The Importance of True Repentance

That's why you shouldn't spare the rod simply because you don't want to hear your child cry. Proverbs 19:18 says, **Chasten thy son while there is hope, and let not thy soul spare for his crying.**

I believe in spanking a child until he cries in repentance. Sometimes while being spanked, a child will have the attitude, *You can spank me as hard as you want to, but I'm not going to cry!* Of course, a child with that kind of attitude is in rebellion.

John Wesley's mother, Susannah Wesley (who was a mother of nineteen and one of the most famous, successful mothers of all time), said this about spanking: "I spank my children until they cry, and then I continue to spank them until they cry softly."[1]

Have you ever heard the rebellious cry of a child? It's a loud cry that makes everyone within earshot take notice of what the parent is doing. The child is trying to cause someone to come and stop the spanking!

---

[1] Adam Clarke, *Memoirs of the Wesley Family* (Hartsville, SC: Vanhooser Publications, 1848), pp. 323, 325.

But a spanking administered in a godly manner will drive that foolishness far from the child. And once a child cries in true repentance, he has submitted himself to receive God-ordained training.

True repentance means the child has turned away from the offense one hundred and eighty degrees, never to do it again. When a child continues to return to the same sin again and again, he never repented in the first place. He just felt sorry that he was caught doing wrong.

God wants your child to learn to be tender and teachable, not hardhearted and rebellious. As you train your child through godly discipline, you will build a sensitivity in him to do what God's Word says to do.

For example, Dea and I designated our bedroom as the special place in the house where discipline with the rod always took place. There were times we would walk by and find one of our boys just standing in that spot, crying.

One time I found Shane there, just weeping his little heart out. I asked him, "Shane, what's wrong?"

"Daddy, I was down the street playing, and I said a naughty word!"

Now, I knew that if Shane hadn't told me that, I might never have known. I asked him, "Well, what are you here for?"

"My spanking," he answered tearfully.

Why would Shane come to that designated place of discipline for his spanking before I even knew he had done something wrong? Because he had been taught since he was a little child that if he obeyed his parents, he would live long on the earth (Eph. 6:1-3). He had disobeyed his parents, so he wanted me to forgive him, and, most of all, he wanted God to forgive him.

So with Shane already crying in repentance over his sin, should I have gone ahead and spanked him? Yes, I should have.

You see, if I hadn't, Shane might have later stood in that same spot and cried, not out of true repentance for something he did wrong, but in order to manipulate the situation so he wouldn't receive a spanking. So that was a good time for me to remember God's admonition in Proverbs 19:18 to "let not my soul — my mind, will and emotions — spare for his crying"!

When a Child Resists Discipline

What do you do if your child physically resists you when you are trying to give him a spanking? Well, Dea and I experienced times when our sons would try that, even though we taught our children to get ready for a spanking by leaning over on the bed and placing their hands on the bed in front of them.

For instance, Shane went through a period when he would squirm, shield his bottom with his hands and try to run away from me in the middle of a spanking. At times I ended up hitting myself more than I hit his bottom!

Finally, I told him, "Son, here's what is going to happen. I'm not holding on to you anymore. If you put your hands on your bottom, I'm going to spank them too. If you want to run, go ahead and run. But I can outrun you.

"I will spank you all through the house, and I won't quit until you willingly go back to the bedroom. Then we'll catch our breath, and you'll receive your original spanking. So it's up to you, Shane; you have a free will. Do you want a long, drawn-out spanking or a quick, private spanking?"

The next time I spanked Shane, down the hallway he went after the first hit of the paddle, and down the hallway I went after him. Suddenly he just froze. Then he ran right back to the bedroom and bent over in the correct position to receive his spanking. Shane had learned his lesson.

Of course, that's the way the Lord led me to deal with that kind of situation. He may lead you differently, but His instructions will always be in line with God's Word.

Discipline in Faith

If a church places the right priority on the Christian home and on children, then it is very possible that the children will be saved and filled with the Holy Spirit at church. But I will tell you this: The best place for children to get saved and Spirit-filled is at home.

You see, it isn't the job of the church to evangelize your children. It is your responsibility as a parent to exercise your faith for their salvation as you train them in the way they should go.

Someone may say, "It just doesn't make sense to me how spanking my child with a paddle is going to deliver his soul from hell!" Well, God never promised us that all of His commands would make sense to our natural minds. He just tells us to exercise faith.

Hebrews 11:1 says, **Now faith is the substance of things hoped for, the evidence of things not seen.** We have to exercise our faith that when disciplined according to the Word, our children will be saved more quickly than children who are not disciplined correctly.

Are you sitting up late at night worrying about your children that God gave you? Do you think God is worrying about them? No, I guarantee you that He isn't.

I mean, where does our faith begin and where does it stop in regard to our children? We may have a lot of faith to believe God for a new car, but too many of us "faith-filled" parents can't believe God to raise a young lady through puberty and on through high school and college who will choose to stay a virgin until marriage!

"Oh, Brother Sturgeon, that could happen back in the '50s, but not in the '90s!" Who said so? You won't find that kind of reasoning in the Word.

So often we are just too carnal. We listen to worldly parents tell us about all the problems they had raising their children, and then we expect to have the same problems with ours! And sure enough, the devil obliges us and sends the same problem along, only worse. Then we stay up until three in the morning worrying about our children — forgetting that they are God's kids in the first place!

If you're going to stay up at night, at least do something profitable: pray in tongues! Don't pray a lot in your understanding, because if you are anxious about your children, even your prayers will probably be based on your carnal thinking. Instead, build up your faith for your children by praying in the Holy Ghost (Jude 20).

It takes faith to raise children, and faith-filled parents end up raising children of faith. Therefore, fear should have no place in your home. Remember what Job said in Job 3:25: **For the thing which I greatly feared is come upon me.**

Instead of living in constant fear for your children, let Mark 11:22-23 be the standard by which you train them:

> **And Jesus answering saith unto them, Have faith in God. For verily I say unto you, That whosoever shall say unto this mountain, Be thou removed, and be thou cast into the sea; and shall not doubt in his heart, but shall believe that those things which he saith shall come to pass; he shall have whatsoever he saith.**

What's the bottom line? We need to operate in faith *all* the time regarding not only our children, but our spouses, our in-laws, our grandmas, our grandpas, our nieces, our nephews — and certainly regarding ourselves! And as we discipline our children according to our faith in God's Word, that Word will not return void in our children's lives. Their soul *will* be delivered from hell, and they *will* be taught the wisdom of God!

C H A P T E R   5

THE DO'S AND DON'TS OF DISCIPLINE

In two separate references in the New Testament, the Bible admonishes fathers (and the same applies to mothers) not to *provoke* their children.

> **And, ye fathers, *provoke not your children* to wrath: but bring them up in the nurture and admonition of the Lord.**
>
> **Ephesians 6:4**
>
> **Children, obey your parents in all things: for this is well pleasing unto the Lord. Fathers, *provoke not your children to anger*, lest they be discouraged.**
>
> **Colossians 3:20-21**

Let me give you some basic do's and don'ts to help you avoid provoking your child to wrath as you establish godly discipline in your home.

Don't Be Inconsistent

One of the most flagrant ways a parent can provoke his or her children to wrath is to be *inconsistent*. Many parents discipline according to their moods. On their good days, a child can commit an atrocity and not be disciplined at all. On bad days, the same child is spanked for sneezing too loudly!

Of course, this inconsistency in discipline discourages a child. He doesn't know any definite boundaries and will eventually rebel out of pure frustration.

It takes diligence, single-mindedness and singleness of purpose to discipline a child properly. It isn't an easy thing to do. A selfish love wants an easier way, but a person motivated by the love of God is willing to maintain the level of consistency the Word demands.

Discipline of children works. But if parents are not consistent, it won't work. In fact, the situation will only get worse!

We must make a commitment to be consistent in training our children according to the Word. When we are consistent, our children will know they can't get away with doing something they know is wrong.

Suppose you tell your children they are going to receive a spanking if they commit a certain offense. For instance, you may tell them, "From now on, if you do thus-and-so, you're going to get a spanking. And I don't care if Grandma and Grandpa are there. I don't care if Aunt and Uncle are there. I don't care if the pastor is there. I don't care if the President of the United States is there!

"It makes no difference who is present; if you do what I told you not to do, you will still get a spanking. It needs to be done, even if I have to spank you ten or fifteen times during a meal."

Once you tell your children something like that, make sure you do what you said you would do. If your child disobeys, don't put off spanking him because it is inconvenient at the moment. If you put it off, you are being inconsistent.

If your child is young and he commits the offense while you are at someone else's home, you need to take care of the situation as soon as possible. Just take him apart to someplace private and give him the spanking he deserves. Don't wait to discipline him after you get home, or he won't remember what he is receiving a spanking for. Of course, if

your child is older, you can wait until you return home to spank him —
but make sure you don't forget to do it!

When the Sturgeon children were young, my mama would say, "Now,
Chuck, it's all right for them to do that over here at Nanny's house."

I would reply, "No, Mama, if it isn't all right for them to do it at our
house, it isn't all right for them to do it here."

It's inconsistent to allow your children to get away with an offense
at someone else's home or at church that they can't get away with in
their own living room. That's why you should never let anyone — even
a close relative — baby-sit your children who won't discipline them
according to the Word as they are disciplined at home. Just one
overnight stay at the wrong babysitter's house can make a difference
in your child's behavior at home.

Some parents say, "Well, if I start using the rod on my children
every time they deserve it, I will be spanking them all the time!"

These parents may have to spank their children frequently for a
while until the children learn that they mean what they say. But parents
who never stop having to spank their children frequently are parents
who aren't being consistent in their discipline.

If you stay consistent in your discipline of your children, a day will
come when you have trained them so well, you won't have to discipline
them much at all.

Don't Discipline in Anger

Another thing that provokes a child is when the parent *disciplines
him in anger.*

When you get angry, you are more wrong than the child, and any
discipline you administer will only drive the child farther from you. So
if you ever start to discipline your child in anger, stop immediately and

get control of yourself. Ask God to forgive you, and ask your children to forgive you.

After you have calmed down and you are no longer angry, then you can make the time of discipline what it should be — a time of love and forgiveness.

Remember the young boy in devotions? When I was angry with him and jerked him out of the service, the entire school knew that Pastor Sturgeon was fed up with that boy. So the first thing I had to do when we arrived at my office was ask him to forgive me for losing my temper. That surprised him, and my apology opened his heart to receive from me as I read the Word to him on discipline.

Correct Your Child's
Wrong *Thoughts*, *Words* and *Deeds*

The rod of discipline should be used to correct *wrong thoughts, words, and deeds*. When a child commits a trespass in the physical realm, parents are usually quick to deal with the wrong deed. But many parents allow their children to speak words of disrespect about them or about other authority figures — words such as "my old man"; "that dumb teacher"; or "the rules of this school are stupid." If parents would stop a child from speaking wrong words, many wrong deeds would never manifest.

The thought realm of a child is the responsibility of his parents too. *Thoughts are powerful.* They determine a person's actions. That's why it is so important to teach your child to think on good things.

And whatsoever ye do in word or deed, do all in the name of the Lord Jesus, giving thanks to God and the Father by him.

Colossians 3:17

Finally, brethren, whatsoever things are true, whatsoever things are honest, whatsoever things are just, whatsoever things are pure, whatsoever things

are lovely, whatsoever things are of good report; if there be any virtue, and if there be any praise, think on these things.

Philippians 4:8

If you will learn to yield to the Lord, at times He will let you know your child's thoughts through the gifts of the Spirit. For example, as my sons were growing up, I would sometimes know by the Spirit what one of them was thinking. Right then I would take him to the bedroom and tell him God had shown me that he had some "stinking thinking." We would talk about what he had been thinking, and, if necessary, I would administer the rod.

I will never forget the time I was walking down the hall of our home, and suddenly I heard what our oldest son, Mike, was thinking just as clearly as if he had spoken it. It stopped me right in my tracks. I turned around and said to him, "Michael Allen Sturgeon, I know exactly what ungodly thoughts you were just thinking! And so that I won't discipline you for the wrong thing, I want you to tell me exactly what you were thinking just now."

Mike told me, and it was precisely what I had heard in the Spirit through the gifts of the Spirit. I spanked him for it, and that was the end of it.

When a child realizes he can't even get away with thinking bad thoughts, he will learn to cast down imaginations and take every thought captive to the obedience of the Word (2 Cor. 10:5).

The home is where you should want the gifts of the Spirit to really flow. In fact, the gifts of the Spirit should operate more in your home than in any other area of your life. Thus families like this who attend a local church enhance the moving of the Holy Spirit in that body.

So make it your goal to get your family in order as you discipline your children for wrong thoughts, words and deeds. Do all you can to get everyone saved, filled with the Spirit and walking with the Lord; to learn how to praise and worship the Lord together as a family; and to grow spiritually to the place that you are operating in all nine gifts of the Spirit severally as the Holy Spirit wills. I tell you what, when that is the status of your home, all glory is going to break loose!

There won't be any more fights on the way to and from church. There won't be any more fights all week long! And if the devil cooks up one of his evil schemes, your entire family can get together and tell him, "In the name of Jesus, get out of here!"

Treat Each Child Equally

When you have more than one child, *treat them equally* in giving love and in disciplining. When you are more lenient with one child than with another, you will discourage the one with whom you are more strict.

If you let one child have a privilege that you forbid to the others, explain to the other children why you are doing it. Let them know that the child who is being given the privilege has shown he can act responsibly in that area.

For example, if you have more than one teenager and one is given the privilege of driving the family car before the others, be sure your teenage children understand that you have given their sibling this privilege because he has demonstrated the necessary maturity to do so — not because you love him more.

When you treat your children equally, they will become equally responsible and well-disciplined. When parents have both obedient and disobedient children, it is probable that they have treated their children differently.

Modern psychology sometimes recommends that parents treat children differently according to their personalities. But God's Word provides only one type of discipline for every child.

Don't Allow Your Children
To Despise Chastening

The Bible makes it very clear that your child must be trained not to despise chastening:

> **My son, despise not the chastening of the Lord; neither be weary of his correction: For whom the Lord loveth he correcteth; even as a father the son in whom he delighteth.**
>
> **Proverbs 3:11-12**
>
> **My son, attend unto my wisdom, and bow thine ear to my understanding. Lest thou give thine honour unto others, and thy years unto the cruel. And say, How have I hated instruction, and my heart despised reproof.**
>
> **Proverbs 5:1, 9, 12**

Don't allow your children to despise the discipline you give them. Always be positive and reinforce the idea that chastening is an element of loving them.

How do you do that? Well, after giving our boys a spanking, Dea and I would tell them, "All right, let's pray. Let's ask God to forgive you, and then you should ask Mother and Daddy to forgive you." Then after praying with them, we would hug and love on them.

At that point, it was all over with; there wouldn't be any more discipline for that particular offense. We didn't take away their bicycle or other privileges. That would have been punishment, not discipline.

You see, when you mess up and ask God to forgive you after being chastened by the Lord through His Word, He forgives you. Then He cleanses you by the blood of Jesus and forgets that you ever committed the sin. He doesn't take your car away from you. He doesn't slap you way out into eternity and then let you find your way back. That may sound silly, but many Christians have this misperception of the way God deals with His children.

So don't take privileges away from your children as a method of disciplining them for disobedience. That could provoke them to wrath and cause them to despise chastening. From your children's perspective, it would seem as if you were always taking something important away from them. The separation from God's fellowship through disobedience should trigger their desire for discipline to put things in right order again. Children like being told by love what they can and cannot do.

Don't Allow Your Children To Rebel

You just can't allow rebellion to live in your house if you want to have a godly family. So for the sake of the entire family, never allow your child to rebel.

For rebellion is as the sin of witchcraft, and stubbornness is as iniquity and idolatry.
1 Samuel 15:23

I took that Scripture seriously in raising my sons. For example, I often had to travel away from the family to minister as my boys were going through their adolescent years. I used to tell them, "Now, listen, boys, I know you're growing up. I know you're bigger than your mother. But when Mom says, 'Go back to the bedroom, lean over and receive your spanking,' you had better do it!

"No meeting is important enough to allow rebellion to reign in our home," I stressed to my sons. "If Mama calls me while I'm away and says that you told her, 'I'm bigger than you are; you're not spanking me anymore,' rest assured that I will cancel the meeting and be on the next plane. And I promise you, when I arrive home, we'll get rid of that rebellion!"

One aspect of keeping rebellion out of your home is teaching your children to respect the authority that God has placed over them in the home, school, community and nation. Discipline them for disrespect-ful attitudes as well as for disobedience.

Remember, too, that you are the standard your children will look to in dealing with life. If you want them to have respect for authority, you must also show respect.

Let every soul be subject unto the higher powers. For there is no power but of God: the powers that be are ordained of God.

Whosoever therefore resisteth the power, resisteth the ordinance of God: and they that resist shall receive to themselves damnation.

Romans 13:1-2

If the law says to drive fifty-five miles per hour, you can be certain that your children will notice if you drive sixty-five miles per hour. And if Daddy can break the law, then it must be okay for everyone else to break it!

If Dad brings home small items from the factory, Junior may begin to bring home little things that he picked up at the store or at the neighbors' house. If Mom dents the car and disclaims any knowledge of it, Suzy will see that it is all right to lie, as long as a person doesn't get caught. (And then parents wonder why their children do what they do!)

That isn't the way it should be. Parents should act honorably at all times in order to be worthy of receiving their children's respect and honor.

The Consequences of Neglecting Discipline

There are often grave consequences when parents don't deal with rebellion in their children through godly discipline. For example, I once had a grandmother in my congregation who was trying to raise her grandson because the parents had failed in their parental responsibili-ties. This teenage boy would actually beat his grandmother when he was upset. When she would try to call me or the police for help, he would rip the phone off the wall.

One night when this woman's grandson was on the rampage, she was able to go next door and call me. I told her, "That grandson of yours has beat you up for the last time. He will never do it again."

"What are we going to do?" she asked.

"Well, I'm your pastor," I said. "So I'm coming over there to pack up his clothes, throw them out the door and kick him out of the house!"

When I arrived at the house, I saw the teenager run out the back door. I drove a white car that looked something like our town's white police cars. The boy probably thought the police had come, so he ran.

I walked in and asked the grandmother, "Where are his clothes?" Then I strode into the bedroom she pointed out and started to fill every container I could find with clothes, throwing them out the front door.

When the teenage boy realized that I wasn't the police and that I was throwing his clothes out the door, he came in and said to me, "Hey! You can't do that!"

His protests didn't bother me a bit. "Listen, Son," I replied, "I'm a child of the Most High God. If Elijah can gird up his loins and outrun the king's horses, I can outrun you until you get tired and then turn around and beat you in a fight!"

I continued, "You have beat up your grandmother for the last time. You aren't going to do it anymore. And you aren't living in this house anymore unless you repent, get saved and filled with the Holy Ghost and speak with other tongues before I leave this house. Otherwise, you're out the door. The locks will be changed, and I'll stay here until they are!"

He said, "You can't make me leave."

"I'm telling you, Son, the only way I'll allow you to stay with your grandma is for you to go over to that divan and start crying out to God right now!"

The boy looked over at the divan — and then he walked over to it and knelt down! I made sure he was really crying out to God before I went over to help him.

When I left that house two hours later , that teenage boy had a recreated spirit and a repentant heart, and he was speaking in tongues. I didn't have to outrun him or anything! Sometimes as a pastor, you just have to do what you have to do!

Remember: There isn't a teenager or child living in your home that you can't control when you are saved and filled with the Holy Ghost. God has given you the power and authority to take care of every situation. So don't let the devil influence your children until they run over you and start telling *you* what to do. Stand in your rightful place as a parent and say, "No, you *are* going to church, young man, even if I have to drag you! In the name of Jesus, you're going! As long as you live in this house, you're going."

I remember another situation in our church where serious consequences resulted from a lack of child discipline. A sixteen-year-old girl — a member of our church and a student in our Christian school — decided she wasn't going to receive spankings from her mother anymore. So she grabbed a Pyrex mixing bowl and hit her mother in the head with it, breaking her mother's glasses and giving her a concussion.

I was in the middle of preaching a sermon when the mother called from the hospital to tell me what happened. She said, "Brother Sturgeon, I've just been doing what you told me to do."

I replied, "No, Sister, you haven't."

"What do you mean?" she asked.

"Well, first of all, have you been consistent in disciplining your daughter?"

The mother didn't have an answer for me. Then I told her, "I'm going to pray with you, and God is going to heal your concussion. And when you get out of that hospital, I want you to bring your daughter over to my office."

So the woman brought her daughter over as soon as she came home from the hospital. I spent a good amount of time reading Scriptures on disciplining a child to the girl without her mother present. I didn't explain the Scriptures to her; I just read them. By the end of that time, that sixteen-year-old girl was standing there weeping! Then I brought the mother in and read the same Scriptures to her. Soon the mother was weeping as well.

I turned to the girl and asked, "What do you deserve?"

"A spanking," she tearfully replied.

"That's right," I said. "Don't ever do anything like that to your mother again."

Then the girl and her mother talked things over. The daughter said, "Mother, I never believed you loved me."

"Why, I've always let you do whatever you wanted to do!" the mother protested.

"That's just it, Mama," the girl said. "My friends are told when they have to come home. But I don't even have to come home! You never tell me what I can and can't do. My friends have to tell their parents when they're coming home and who they're going out with. You never even ask. I thought it was because you didn't care. I didn't believe you loved me."

According to the Word, if parents spare the rod, they hate their children (Prov. 13:24). Therefore, that woman hated her daughter. She didn't love her the way God commanded her to love her daughter. Hate and love don't mix.

But both daughter and mother repented that day, and they straightened out some things in their relationship. And the daughter is still serving God to this day. The Word does make a difference!

Listen, friend, if you allow rebellion in your home by neglecting to discipline your child the way you should, a day *will* come when *someone* will tell your child what he can and cannot do — and it may be someone with a badge and a gun!

Most of those in the penitentiary today were raised by parents who never loved and respected them enough to discipline them. That's so sad.

When you allow your children to get away with rebellion in the home, you are as wrong as your children are. And if you allow them to continue to live that way until they grow to adulthood and leave home to live on their own, somewhere down the line there will be a payday. Rebellion *always* brings negative consequences.

Personally, I would rather make the effort to discipline my children and do what God's Word tells me to do while they are still at home. I don't want to see them learn the hard way by living a life of havoc somewhere out in the future. That's why rebellion was never allowed to live in our home for even a moment.

More Discipline Mistakes To Avoid

Here's a few more "don'ts" to remember as you learn to discipline your children God's way:

Don't allow your children to complain. Complaining and grumbling is a big deal to God. Numbers 11:1 says, **And when the people complained,**

it displeased the Lord. Through complaining and unbelief, the Israelites lost their opportunity to enter the Promised Land.

Don't allow your children to be bitter. A root of bitterness that is allowed to grow inside your child can adversely affect not only his own life, but the lives of those around him. Hebrews 12:15 says this:

> **Looking diligently lest any man fail of the grace of God; lest any root of bitterness springing up trouble you, and thereby many be defiled.**

Even if a child is wrongfully condemned by someone, a root of bitterness should never be allowed to lodge in his heart against that person. Teach your child to walk in forgiveness toward everyone.

If your child wants to complain about a person or a situation, instruct him to speak his *faith* about it instead. Tell him to call things that are not as though they were. If the situation or person is wrong, God will move on your child's behalf as he chooses to forgive.

Don't allow your child to be slothful or wasteful. Teach him to be a good steward of his time, money and possessions. Proverbs 18:9 says, **He also that is slothful in his work is brother to him that is a great waster.**

Waster in the Hebrew means "destroyer." Satan is the destroyer. The more irresponsible a person is with time and money, the more he opens himself to Satan's ravages and shuts himself off from God's blessings.

Don't make your child do something you won't do yourself. Always be sure your instructions are in line with the Word. Ephesians says to obey your parents "in the Lord." If you act in a way that is not in line with the Word, train your child well enough to recognize it. And when he sets you straight, ask him to forgive you.

Don't ridicule, belittle, scorn or embarrass your child. Love is supposed to *edify* and *encourage* a person to achieve his fullest potential, not tear him down.

Avoid spanking your child in public, especially in front of his peers. Always take him apart from the others to administer discipline. The friends may hear your child crying, but at least he will know you respected his desire not to be embarrassed in front of them.

Always have a compliment for your child, especially after disciplining him. Even if you have a difficult time thinking of something positive at the moment, find *something* to mention that will build up your child's self-esteem.

For example, when we first started our Christian school, we held classes in a hotel. One day one of our young boys threw hard-boiled eggs out the window and poured water on the people sitting a floor below in the lobby. Of course, this kind of behavior didn't do much for school-hotel relations!

When I finished spanking this boy, it was a real challenge to find something to compliment him about. Finally, I told him that he certainly wore his uniform neatly. The boy walked away chastened but with his confidence built up because he looked good.

Once this boy knew he could please us, he began to try to do well overall in school. We didn't have much more trouble with that little boy. He always stood out among the others with the neatest and cleanest uniform.

Train Your Child To *Do* the Word

Sometimes parents "overplan" their child's life. Parents need to operate in the wisdom of God to know when to make decisions for the child and when to let him work out a problem for himself. The parents' job is to train the child in the way he should go so that when it's time, he can go that way on his own.

Once you teach your child what the Word says about an area of his life, train him to *do* the Word. For instance, once he learns the truths in

Luke 6:38 and Malachi 3:10, train him to tithe, give and believe God for a return.

When my oldest son, Mike, was growing up, he was always diligent to tithe and give of his money to God's kingdom. One summer he wanted extra money, so he decided to mow lawns. However, he had a problem — he didn't have a lawn mower!

One day a man down the street who had never been to our house came to see Mike. This man owned quite a bit of rental property around town. He told Mike that he wanted him to mow all of his lawns. The man also said he would supply the mower, the gas and drive him to and from jobs for Mike was too young to drive. God provided for Mike because he was a faithful giver!

All of my sons learned to apply their faith in other areas as well. Dea and I taught our sons since they were little boys, "We'll give you gifts at Christmas, and we'll give you gifts on your birthday. We love to give gifts to you and make you happy. But when it comes to something big that you want, you'll have to believe God for it."

And they did! At different times as they were growing up, they believed God for a horse, a bicycle, a minibike, and even a round trip airplane flight —and received them all!

Over the years I have learned to trust my sons' faith. I like to have them pray the prayer of agreement with me about important matters. I have heard my sons pray, and I have seen the results of those prayers.

For example, when Mike was nine, we lived on the homestead where my grandfather used to raise draft horses. The old barn and horse stalls were still standing.

Well, Mike got hold of the Word and decided to believe God for a horse. When the family would arrive home from a ministry trip, Mike's first thought would be to run out to the barn and turn on the lights, even if it was two o'clock in the morning. He *expected* that horse to be there.

Every time Mike ran out to the barn, I would prepare myself to wipe away his tears when he came back to report that no horse was there. But every time, he would return with a smile on his face. He never gave up on the horse he was believing for.

Then God moved us to town. One night I asked Mike to pray over the evening meal. After thanking the Lord for the food, he said, "And, Father, I thank You for my horse."

I thought, *Well, I better talk to this boy about this. We live in town now, and we don't have a place to keep a horse.* So I took Mike aside and said, "Son, you have to realize that we don't have a place to put a horse anymore."

Tears came to Mike's eyes, and he said, "Daddy, I've already seen my horse. I know exactly what he looks like. He's mine!"

Well, I thought, *I can't talk him out of it. Someday when he's an adult, he'll give up.*

Less than a year later, a man came to us and said, "Before I give this to your boys, I want to ask your permission."

"Well, what is it?" I asked.

"A horse," he replied.

Mike received his answer to prayer! I thought in amazement. Out loud I said, "Well, I can't deny the boys that! But where am I going to put a horse?"

"In my stable," the man said. "You see, I own a stable, and I want to give your boys a horse. I bought them a bridle and saddle. I'll buy all the oats and hay. All they will have to do is feed and water it and ride it whenever they want to."

That happened because of nine-year-old Mike's faith — and he was just getting started! When he graduated from high school, he set his faith on a new pickup truck.

I told Mike, "Now, Son, I just want to let you know that I'm not buying you a truck. I'm not cosigning on a note for you either. You'll have to believe God for it on your own."

Mike answered (not out of disrespect, but in a matter-of-fact manner), "Daddy, I didn't expect you to." He had already put out his faith for the vehicle he wanted.

Soon after Mike graduated from high school, a woman we knew who lived outside of town unexpectedly dropped by for a visit. She and I sat down with a cup of coffee to talk.

The woman asked, "Where's Michael?"

"He's out looking for a new pickup truck."

"Oh, is he?" she said. "Well, what is Mike going to do now that he has graduated from high school?"

"I don't really know," I said. "But I know he's out looking for a new pickup. I encouraged him to look at used ones, but he is looking at new ones."

That's all I said about the subject. The woman finished her cup of coffee and then got up to leave.

About two hours later, the same woman returned. She said, "You said that Michael was out looking for a pickup."

"That's right."

"Has he found one yet?" she asked.

"Well," I replied, "he hasn't come home with a new pickup yet."

"Okay," the woman said, "would you just give him this and tell him to buy a good one?" Then she handed a check to me, made out to Michael Allen Sturgeon for ten thousand dollars!

Could I tell my son he couldn't have that brand new pickup truck? Of course not — no more than I could have told him at nine years old that he couldn't have the horse he had believed for!

But I was stunned. I asked the woman, "Are you sure?" I mean, at this point I wanted to receive counsel from my own son on how to stand in faith for something!

Now, why did things like that happen in our household as the boys were growing up? Did they happen because I was in the ministry? No, our sons received supernatural answers to prayer because the Word of God had been planted in their hearts, and they had been trained to not only believe God's Word, but to *do* it. That's the best insurance policy for a successful life in God that we could have ever given our boys.

We also taught the boys how to act on the Word to receive physical healing. For instance, even before Shane was saved and Spirit-filled at age four, he knew that if Mama and Daddy prayed for him, his tummy-ache or headache would leave. Whatever was hurting in his little body, he knew it would leave.

So Shane would run to us and ask us to lay hands on him and pray. If he had a fever, we could actually feel the fever leave as we prayed. Then Shane would turn right around and run back outside to play. Now, as his parents, our natural inclination was to have him lie down while we prayed real hard. But Shane would just simply receive his healing like it was no big deal.

When the boys reached school age, I'd tell them, "Don't think you're going to get up one morning and say, 'I'm going to stay home from school today because I'm sick.' Sickness and disease don't belong in this house. So if you wake up with symptoms, you had better start believing God.

"You aren't going to lie around the house pampering sickness. You know how to receive your healing by faith. So just get out of bed and go eat your breakfast, thanking God for your healing. And before you walk out of the house for school, you'll be healed."

We could make such a strong requirement of their faith because we had taught and trained them to believe and act on the Word. They had already experienced supernatural answers to their own prayers. Each parent needs to be confident that his or her child is spiritually equipped to stand in faith for his or her healing.

Some people think I was being hard on my sons. But Dea and I had determined that we were going to kick the devil out of our home. To accomplish that, we couldn't just tolerate the presence of sickness in the home; we had to go after it with our faith. I wasn't being hard on the boys; I was being hard on the devil!

Besides, I gave the boys a reward for believing God for their healing. I told them. "One of these days I'll give you a day off from school for being well! We may go fishing or hunting, or you can spend the whole day playing. You see, you can't enjoy staying home from school when you're sick. But when you earn a day off for being well, you *can* enjoy it!"

I was true to my word. One of the days we generally took off was the day all the schools celebrated Halloween. Our boys would make sure they were out in front of the house playing when the other children walked home from school to eat their lunch.

The children would ask our sons, "What are you doing at home instead of at school? Are you sick?"

The boys would reply, "No, Dad let us stay home because we're well!" After that, the Sturgeon family would often go to the ranch for the afternoon or somewhere else for a family outing. The boys liked their reward for walking in divine health!

You may say, "That's a different approach." Well, we in the body of Christ ought to be different, as long as it is according to God's Word!

So teach your children that Jesus gives all good gifts and that *their* faith will work for them.

Benefits of Godly Discipline

Many parents don't want to hear about the do's and don'ts of discipline. They don't like all the rules God wants them to enforce. "I want my child to be free," they declare.

But real freedom is gained when children have learned to receive God's direct guidance. Psalm 119:45 says, **And I will walk at liberty: for I seek thy precepts.**

Some people are actually in bondage to freedom! They flitter around being "free," but they neglect to *do* the Word — and they usually end up with their lives in a confused mess.

On the other hand, children who are disciplined according the Word as they grow into adulthood reap a great many benefits. For one thing, as they learn to believe and do the Word of God, they become *wise in the affairs of life.*

Also, an obedient child will enjoy a *long life.*

> **Children, obey your parents in the Lord: for this is right. Honour thy father and mother; which is the first commandment with promise; That it may be well with thee, and *thou mayest live long on the earth.***
>
> **Ephesians 6:1-3**

Disobedience to parental authority is one reason why life spans became shorter in the Old Testament. God promises His protection to a person who learns to obey his parents.

Any parent who loves his child desires God's protective power operating in the child's life. Well, training him to be an obedient child is a sure way to fulfill that desire!

When you discipline your child according to God's Word, the child will begin to *discipline himself.* A self-disciplined person is a successful person in every area of life. It takes self-discipline to get up in the morning, to hold a steady job, to serve God diligently. The sooner a child learns to control himself, the more capable he will be of dealing with the responsibilities of life.

A home containing well-disciplined children is a restful situation. Proverbs 29:17 says, **Correct thy son, and he shall give thee rest; yea, he shall give delight unto thy soul.** Most people today are not delighted or at rest about their children. In fact, the average parents are worried to distraction about them. They are actually in fear about what Junior may do next to shame them. It is *not* a restful situation.

But if your child is well-disciplined, you know he will bring you no shame. You know that even when he is away from your presence, he is doing only good things and earning a good reputation.

It is an honor to have an obedient child. People will love to come to your home because of the peace and rest in it. You won't have to point out your child's good behavior. If they have been trained according to the Word of God, people will notice the difference.

Proverbs 20:11 says it this way: **Even a child is known by his doings, whether his work be pure, and whether it be right.** When your child's "work" is pure and right, you can delight in him and be at rest.

The Bible promises that **the father of a righteous man has great joy; he who has a wise son delights in him** (Prov. 23:24, NIV). You see, there isn't anything quite like hearing people say something wonderful about your child and knowing it is true because you have done what God's Word says you should do as a parent. After fulfilling your parental responsibilities to discipline your child, you receive the parental joy of living with an obedient child!

When To Start and Stop Disciplining

People sometimes ask me, "When is the best time to start training a child?" They are often surprised by my answer: "The best time to start training up a child in the way he should go is at the time of conception!"

Why is that? Because your child is an immortal spirit being. A spirit never grows old and never dies. Once that child is conceived, one of two things can happen: He can be born into this world, receive Jesus as his Savior, live his life for God and go on to enjoy everlasting life with Jesus Christ. Or he can choose to live a life of sin and never receive Jesus, only to die and spend an eternity in hell.

The stakes are too high to neglect the training of our children — and the sooner we start, the better.

So how do you start training your child from conception on? Well, we used to tell the young mothers in our congregation, "Mama, during the course of the nine months you carry that baby in your womb, sit down and read the entire Word of God to him. Say out loud, "Honey, perk up your ears now and listen to Mama. I'm going to read to you from God's Word. This is what Jesus has to say."

Then we told the husbands, "Now, listen, we know that you're busy being the breadwinner of the family. But nothing is more important than this child of yours.

"So when you come home at night, lay your hand on your wife's womb and speak to your baby. It doesn't make any difference whether it's a girl or a boy; just say to your unborn child, 'Now, listen here, Sweetheart, perk up your ears and listen while Daddy reads the Word to you.'

"Then proceed to read the entire Bible to that child during the course of the nine months he is in your wife's womb. As you and your wife are faithful to train your child in the Word from the time of conception , we will guarantee you this: Whether the child is inside or outside the womb, you will be able to tell him what he can and cannot do, and he will listen to you."

Parents have tested and proven that counsel many times over the years. For example, a young couple named Frank and Gayla who attended our Bible training center conceived a child just before the beginning of the school year. Therefore, Gayla's due date came near the end of the school year.

So all through the pregnancy, the baby growing inside this young mother's womb heard the teaching of the Word of God. Her unborn child's little spirit just soaked up the Word.

One Friday near the end of the school year, Gayla left class to have her baby, and she was back on Monday with baby Simon! We put him in a little bassinet in the classroom, and he was never any problem. Gayla would talk to her infant son just as if he could understand her — because his spirit could! He had been taught of the Lord the entire time he was in the womb, and the Word will not return void.

Gayla would wake her baby up in the morning and say, "Sweetheart, it's time to get up; we have to go to school. You're going to nurse now." And little Simon would always do just as his mother said.

Or Gayla would say, "We're on our way to school now, Son. When we arrive there, we'll praise and worship the Lord for thirty minutes and then have two hours of classes. After that, you and I will go to the intercessory prayer room, and you'll nurse then. So remember, you can't cry and make a fuss during class."

I want you to know that Simon cried out loud only *one time* in all the weeks he lay there in the bassinet during class — from eight o'clock to noon every day, five days a week! The one time Simon did cry the students were taking a test, so I went back and picked him up. I tried everything I knew to do to stop his crying, but he wouldn't stop.

Then one of the students said, "I know what the problem is. When the Word goes forth, Simon is peaceful and restful. But you gave us this ungodly test!" Everyone had a good laugh, and Simon soon calmed down.

But that was the only time Simon cried in class. That little baby would do exactly what his parents told him to do. He would nurse when his mother said to nurse; he would go to bed when she said to go to bed. He didn't get his days and nights mixed up. Mom and Dad would tell him, "This is the way it is," and from his first day out of the womb, Simon obeyed what they told him to do.

So when school ended that year and Simon's parents graduated, we gave Simon a diploma too! We figured that since he had attended the training center through the entire year and had kept a perfect attendance record either inside or outside the womb, he had earned that diploma!

As Simon grew into the toddler years, he continued to be an obedient child. For instance, he and his parents would sometimes visit us at our home. All of our boys were older at the time, so we didn't have many toys in our house for toddlers to play with. Not only that, but Dea had a lot of objects — plants, vases and so forth — that a toddler isn't supposed to touch.

But that wasn't a problem with Simon. He would walk over and look at one of those forbidden objects; then he would look at his parents. When they said, "No, Simon," he would turn and look at the tempting object as if to say, "Well, it looks like it would have been fun to play with." Then he'd just obediently walk away from it.

This young family lived in a mobile home, and Simon's bedroom was located in the back of the trailer. One night Frank and Gayla were watching a movie in the living room (which was on the other end of the mobile home) while Simon played in his bedroom.

The movie had started well, capturing the couple's interest. But then about halfway through it, the moral quality of the movie started going downhill fast. But because they wanted to know how the plot turned out, Frank and Gayla decided they were "mature" enough to watch it to the end.

Suddenly little Simon, who had just learned to walk, toddled into the living room all the way from the back of the trailer. And to his parents' surprise, he went over to the television set, pushed the power button with his little finger and turned it off! Then he turned around and headed right back to his bedroom, where he resumed playing again.

Frank and Gayla looked at each other, thinking, *Surely Simon didn't do that deliberately because he knew that movie wasn't a good one to watch!* So they went back to Simon's bedroom and looked in. There he was, happily playing with his toys, his back to the door.

So Mom and Dad snuck back to the living room, turned the television back on with the volume set low and began to watch the movie again. All of a sudden, Simon reappeared, toddled over to the television and turned it off again! This time Simon's mom and dad took the hint and gave up on watching the movie.

What did that little child sense in the Spirit? The spiritual garbage that was coming out of that television tube! Remember, he had been taught of the Lord since conception!

Later Simon and his parents moved about eighty miles away from us, and we didn't see them for five years. But one day Dea and I were eating in a restaurant, and I happened to look over at a nearby booth. There were Frank, Gayla and Simon!

Simon hadn't seen me in five years. But the moment he caught sight of me in the restaurant, his eyes lit up. Immediately he jumped out of that booth, ran over and gave me a hug. I had taught him the Word of God while he was in the womb, and he wasn't afraid of me. In the natural he may have forgotten who I was, but his spirit recognized me.

That's just one of the many testimonies I could tell you of parents who have ministered God's Word to their children since the time of conception. Because these parents were obedient to God, they are now reaping the reward of having obedient children.

Once a couple knows that the wife is pregnant, both the husband and wife should begin to minister God's Word to the child in the womb. If they will start that practice early and do it consistently, it will reap wonderful rewards for a lifetime!

When Is a Child 'Old'?

We have been "going down the trail" of Proverbs to see what God has to say about child discipline. Proverbs 22:6 gives us more valuable insight:

Train up a child in the way he should go: and when he is old, he will not depart from it.

I have heard people say, "Yes, somewhere in the 'sweet bye-and-bye' when my children are old — sometime before they die — they will come back to God." No, that isn't what this verse means.

Once when I was meditating on this Scripture, I asked the Lord, "When is a child old?" I was thinking, *Well, maybe if the child strays from God, he'll return to Him by the time he's in his eighties or nineties.*

But the Lord spoke to my heart, saying, "No, a child is no longer a child in the real sense of the word after he reaches the age of puberty, because at that point he has attained physical maturity. At the age of puberty, a little child is no longer a little child, because he or she can physically do anything an adult can do.

"When a little boy's loins come alive so that he is capable of impregnating a womb, he is no longer a little boy; he is a young man. And a little girl is no longer a little girl when she is capable of conceiving a child in her womb from the union of a lively sperm and a lively egg; she is now a young woman."

"If that's true, Lord," I replied, "then what are You telling me?"

"If parents want My best," the Lord told me, "they should train their children from conception to puberty. The training or discipline of a child ought to be essentially complete by the time of puberty.

"When your child reaches the teenage years, you ought to have a child whom you can trust because he has the Word in him. You should be able to stand in faith on the training your teenager has already received and say to him, 'I have faith in you. You're a disciple taught of the Lord.'

"And when your child is old enough to drive, you should be able to reach in your pocket and say, 'Here are the keys. Go out and have a good time. I just want you back home by a certain time.' You should have no concern at all about what your teenager might do with the family car."

When are we able to trust our teenage children like that? After we have trained them in the admonition of the Lord, so that when they are old, they will not depart from the truth they have learned.

One of the most common worries parents experience with their teenagers is what will happen when they are out with the opposite sex. But when parents train their children right, they will be able to trust them in that area.

I remember the big change regarding girls that occurred when each of my three sons reached the age of puberty. When the boys were young and we visited other churches, they would often kick up a dust cloud around the church as six or seven little girls chased them. I never will forget the time I rescued Shane from a little girl who was dragging him up the church stairs!

But that all changed as the boys grew older. Before long, we saw *our boys* chasing the *girls* around the church. Then after the boys hit puberty, we would find them holding hands with girls they had never seen before!

We had a memorable moment the summer my youngest son Shane reached puberty. He and his brothers went to church camp as they did every summer. On the way home from camp, I asked the boys the same question I asked every year: "What was something that meant a lot to you this year?" I knew something was different when it was Shane's turn to reply, and he said, "There were a lot of girls in camp this year."

Brian said, "Shane, there have always been a lot of girls at camp!" But Shane had just started noticing them. All of a sudden, girls weren't "yucky" anymore!

When we first witnessed these changes in the boys, Dea and I thought, *Dear God, what's happening?* But then we realized that the boys were just growing up.

So we stopped treating them like little children. We knew that we had put the Word in our sons since they were very young. So now we stood on our faith in that Word, gradually giving the boys more independence. We knew that the Word of God in their hearts would speak to their conscience, saying, "This isn't right" or "Don't go too far." We put our trust in the power of that Word to keep our sons on course.

Will your children still make mistakes after you have trained them according to the Word? Sure, they will, but not nearly as drastic or as many as you made when you were young if as a child you weren't trained God's way.

Discern Your Child's Divine Call

Another important phrase in Proverbs 22:6 says that you are to train up your child **in the way he should go.** One translation says, **Train up the lad in accordance with his course.**[1]

God has ordained a way, or a course in life, for your child to take. And if you start training him from conception on, you will know the call of God that is on his life — the way he should go — before he is ever born.

God said to Jeremiah, **Before I formed thee in the belly I knew thee; and before thou camest forth out of the womb I sanctified thee, and I ordained thee a prophet unto the nations** (Jer. 1:5). God was telling Jeremiah, "I knew you before you were born. I formed you in your mother's womb. I even ordained you there for the call I have set you apart to fulfill."

You may ask, "Does *every* child have a divine call?" You better believe it! I'm not saying that all children are called to be an apostle, prophet, evangelist, pastor or teacher. But I *am* saying that every child has a call of God on his life, a divine purpose to fulfill.

God has put forth a call to every person ever born on this earth. If you conducted a study on the Hebrew and Greek words for *call, called* and *calling,* you would find out the predominant call that includes all of us is the call of God through the Holy Ghost to receive a Bride for His Son. That is the call of salvation, and it goes out to all men.

You see, God has put within the spirit of every child born from a mother's womb an inborn desire to serve a god. Man will make a god out

---

[1] Isaac Leeser, *Twenty-Four Books of the Holy Scriptures* (New York: Hebrew Publishing Co., n.d.), p. 1106.

of a piece of metal or a piece of wood if he knows of no other God to serve. But countless times throughout the centuries, when people hear about Jesus, they are willing to throw all false gods away. Why? Because they know they have met the real God that they were born to serve.

But besides being called to salvation, every child has also been called to follow a particular course in his life — a course planned by God before the foundations of the earth.

Even parents who aren't born again can usually discern what that course is by observing a child's "bent," or his natural gifts and graces. So if you are saved, Spirit-filled and know how to hear from God, you definitely ought to know in your spirit the course your child's life is supposed to take so you can point him in the right direction.

For example, Dea and I have known from the beginning that our middle son, Brian, is called of God to the music ministry. Brian started to learn about music on a little drum pad when he was just a little boy. He didn't even have a teacher.

From the drum pad, Brian advanced to a snare drum and then on to a trap set. He has played drums in church by the Holy Spirit, and it is a beautiful thing to hear. Brian has also taught others how to play the drums by the Spirit of the Lord.

When Brian was just a baby, he would try to play everything that made any kind of interesting sound. We have a picture of him in his little undershorts, holding a songbook upside down and just singing away. God's call to the music ministry was in him even when he was little.

If you will stay sensitive to the Lord, you, too, will know in your spirit where your children are headed in life as they follow God. It is important that you discern their divine call so you can train and encourage them in the way that they should go, or in the way they are divinely "bent." You can make sure that by the time your children launch out on their own, they are trained to be successful in their God-ordained occupation or calling.

Of course, ultimately, you can't make the decision for your children to obey that call. The older your children get, the more they will want to be responsible for making their own choices. And as long as their choices are in line with God's Word and they aren't doing anything wrong, you shouldn't come against their decisions.

However, your teenage child may begin to make choices that points him in a particular direction that isn't wrong in itself, but that you know in your spirit isn't the course God wants him to take in life. If that happens, just continue to gently point him in the right direction.

When it is appropriate, say things like, "When you were just a little baby, I remember what God told me as I sat nursing you" or "When you were in first grade and I had to walk away and leave you at school for the first time, the Lord said this to me about you" or "I'll never forget the time that minister laid hands on you and prophesied, and God said..."

Just share with your child whatever God has said to you over the years that makes him so special and precious to you. As you do, you will bring back to his remembrance God's perspective of him. You will be keeping God's words before him as he sits, as he walks, as he stands, as he arises and as he goes to sleep. Someday he will think about those words, and they will help him choose the way he should go.

INSTITUTING DIVINE DISCIPLINE

Now that you have studied the *why* and the *how* of divine discipline, you are probably wondering how to institute it into *your* household. If you realize that you have missed God in dealing with your children, don't despair. Your household may be in a mess, but God promises that He can fix even the biggest fiasco.

Once a couple came to me and said, "We stopped spanking our teen two years ago, and since then we have seen more rebellion in him. Is it too late to start spanking again?"

I will tell you the same thing I told that couple: No, it isn't too late. You may have some difficulty in establishing that method of discipline again with your teenager. But as you ask God to forgive you for mishandling your children and believe Him to heal your family, His Word promises that He will!

> **Come, and let us return unto the Lord and he will bind us up.**
>
> **Hosea 6:1**
>
> **And I WILL RESTORE TO YOU THE YEARS that the locust hath eaten, the cankerworm, and the caterpiller, and the palmerworm.**
>
> **Joel 2:25**

I don't know your children or the problems you face with them. I don't know whether you have been married once or twice or three times. But even if I did, I wouldn't say anything different than I am saying now. Does your situation change the Word? Does it make the blood of Jesus less effective?

No, you are still alive. You can still ask forgiveness for your mistakes as a spouse and a parent. The blood is still powerful enough to take care of the situation and to cleanse you from past sins and failures. Thank God for the blood!

So don't feel condemned about the mistakes you have made in the past. God is the God of restoration. When those things you have been believing for in times past are finally manifested in your family, He will make the present so wonderful that you will almost forget the pain of the past. Hearts will be healed, and the times shared with your family will be so precious that it will make up for all those years the devil seemingly stole from you and your children.

Regaining Lost Ground Through Prayer

When parents have lost ground in disciplining their children through inconsistency or neglect, how do they gain back that lost ground? Well, first of all, they must get back to the basics of asking God for forgiveness and then seeking Him in prayer every day.

I know a man who gets up at 4:30 every morning and prays an hour — not for the church he pastors, but for his family. He is faithful to do that no matter how late he goes to bed the night before. Only after he prays for his family does he pray for his church.

(You see, the call of God doesn't negate the minister's duty to make the family his highest priority. Family should never suffer as a result of the minister putting the ministry first. God didn't intend for it to be that way.)

So if you have lost ground, you need to spend time in prayer. Hear from God about how to gain that ground back. It is a good idea to pray

112

much in tongues, for although your mind is unfruitful, you are building up your most holy faith (Jude 20). And as you are faithful to pray, God will tell you what to do.

The Power of Agreement

So what are the steps to take on the road to instituting divine discipline in the home? First, parents should read aloud and study together the Scriptures presented in this book (see pages 169-187). Then they should both make a strong, quality decision to apply those Scriptures to their family.

Both parents must be in total agreement in this matter, or they won't achieve the consistency in discipline their children need. Even if the husband and wife can't agree with everything presented in this book, they must agree with each other and with God's Word if they are going to be effective in disciplining their children.

You may say, "But my spouse and I *don't* fully agree on how to discipline our children." Well, then, institute whatever discipline principles from the Word that you and your spouse *can* agree on.

You don't have to throw the entire book on discipline at your family all at once anyway. If necessary, you can establish godly discipline in your home step by step, a little at a time. Remember, God is love, and love wouldn't tell us to do something that would push our family away from us. The main thing is to begin the process as soon as possible.

You may ask, "But what should I do if my spouse and I disagree about how to discipline our child in a particular situation?" That's not an uncommon situation.

Many times the father is the law of the household, who says, "This is the way it's going to be, or else!" On the other hand, the mother is often stronger in the area of grace.

A sensitivity often exists between the child and his mother that is greater than that which exists between the child and his father. Remember, the mother bore those children through her womb. So when the father starts to spank one of the children, the mother may say, "But he's been such a good boy lately!"

You and your spouse can end up working against each other when you disagree in front of your child about how to discipline him. Those are the times you need retreat for a private conference in your bedchamber, your "love nest," where the children are really not supposed to be. Hold a parents' meeting between the two of you and decide how you will deal with the situation.

How are you going to decide? Find out what the Word says. The Word will bring you both back to reality. Then it isn't "what I think" or "what *you* think," but "What does the Word say?" After your meeting, implement only the discipline you can agree on.

You see, in a marriage relationship, there ought to be mutual submission between one another on important matters. Dea and I don't do anything unless we can agree on it. But when she doesn't know what to do and someone has to make the decision, she just puts herself in agreement with whatever I decide to do. And if my decision turns out to be a wrong one, then we learn from that situation and go on from there.

As Christian husbands and wives, we can tap into Jesus' promise that great power is released through the prayer of agreement:

**Again I say unto you, That if two of you shall agree
on earth as touching any thing that they shall ask, it
shall be done for them of my Father which is in heaven.
Matthew 18:19**

Over the years, Dea and I have called ourselves a "dynamic duo." Why? Because as father and mother, we can grab hold of each other's hands and agree together in the name of Jesus regarding our children, and God will back up His Word.

When one man and one woman make a covenant of agreement with God, it affects all of their children. When Noah made a covenant with God, it affected his children so much that they were saved from destruction. When Abraham made a covenant with God, it affected an entire nation.

How much more should we under the New Covenant be able to believe that our covenant with the Father God through the blood of Jesus Christ affects everyone in our household?

Make a Vow Together

When you and your spouse are certain of the discipline principles on which you can stand solidly together, then make a vow together before God that you will obey His Word in training your children. However, *don't* make this vow if you don't intend to keep it or if you only want to *try* God's way of discipline for a while. Making a vow before the Lord is serious business (Deut. 23:21-23).

Be sure to speak your vow out loud *because your words have creative power.*

> **For verily I say unto you, That whosoever shall say unto this mountain, Be thou removed, and be thou cast into the sea; and shall not doubt in his heart, but shall believe that those things which he saith shall come to pass; *he shall have whatsoever he saith.***
>
> **Mark 11:23**

Make an Appointment With Your Children

After you and your spouse have told God that you are serious about training your children His way, arrange a meeting with your children.

Make it a special, uninterrupted session. Turn off the television, and let the answering machine take your telephone calls.

Then create an enjoyable atmosphere. Do something the family likes to do together. For instance, pop some popcorn and sit around the fireplace as you read the Word of God to your children.

Take time to go through the Scriptures on child discipline with your children, explaining what the verses mean and how they apply to your children's lives. However, don't try to teach or preach to them. Just read the Scriptures, making sure they understand that this is God's perfect way of disciplining children and that you desire to please Him in this area. Then give your children an opportunity to ask questions. Let them talk to you and tell you how they feel about the subject.

Next, ask your children to forgive you. Tell them, "As parents, we want to ask you to forgive us. We failed both God and you in this area of discipline. From now on, we're going to institute the paddle as God's method of discipline in this family."

It means a lot to children when their parents admit they made a mistake and apologize to them. For example, I always knew I was in trouble when my son Brian would come into my office and ask for a copy of my little book *Train Up a Child* (a former, smaller version of this book). I would give Brian a copy of the book, knowing that he wasn't asking for it so he could give it to someone else.

Brian would leave for a while, but soon he would return and say something like, "Dad, on page 17, paragraph four, it says that 'Brow-beating will never replace bottom beating.' Dad, when you said..." Then Brian would explain to me how something I had said to him had hurt him. What would I do at a time like that? I'd asked Brian for forgiveness.

After asking your children to forgive you, have a time of prayer together in which you ask God to forgive you as well. Then firmly lay down the basics.

You may want to say something like this: "Kids, from now on when you do something wrong, we aren't going to yell and scream at you. We will just tell you in a normal tone what we expect of you. For instance, we might tell you to empty the trash. If you don't empty the trash, then we will give you swats for it. We will always do it in your bedroom, and here is the instrument that we will spank you with. It's just that simple.

"God is a God of love, and He told us to do this; therefore, this is what we're going to do. Since you are obedient children, we know you are going to submit yourselves totally to God's way of discipline. And because we're all going to obey God, this family will be blessed because of it!"

As you lay down the rules, do it in love. Don't act like a general in the army, listing so many rules that you stifle your children or put them in fear. Remember that God's way is love's way.

Be sure to *write down your rules* so every family member has a clear idea of what the rules are. Start small; don't make any rules you won't enforce. Also, don't expect too much of your children. A six-year-old can't perform on the level of a ten-year-old. Besides, you need to remember that it was your neglect of doing the Word in the area of discipline that has caused them to be less than the obedient children they are supposed to be. Therefore, *be reasonable.*

Enforce Consistently

When your meeting with your children is over, don't try to play "catch-up" for your past leniency by spanking them for previous offenses. That *isn't* the way to begin! Start fresh on the night of the meeting, after you are sure that your children have a good understanding of the new set of ground rules for discipline in the home.

Once you have made it clear to your children what discipline according to the Word means, you must enforce that discipline consistently.

The first few days you may find yourself using the rod frequently. But after a few days of this, your children will begin to see that you mean business, and the number of spankings will decrease markedly.

The Proper Procedure for Discipline

Remember that training involves love as well as control. The time you take a disobedient child back to the particular room you have designated as the room for discipline must be a time of love *and* control.

Let's take a closer look at what should go on in this room.

First of all, make sure your child understands what wrong he has committed and why he is receiving discipline at this time. Have him explain to you the nature of his offense.

Train your child to submit to the spanking willingly. If he is very young, you can lean him over your lap. An older child should bend over with his hands placed on something in front of him, such as the back of a chair or the bed.

Tell your child to keep his hands away from his bottom. If he still tries to shield his bottom with his hands, keep spanking. You can pray for his hands later; meanwhile, he will learn to submit to the spanking.

After you have used the rod and your child has totally submitted to it, end the time of discipline in prayer. Instruct the child to ask God to forgive him. Then *you* pray. Confess the Word that is working in your child's life.

Finally, show your love for him. Hug or hold him, and tell him that you love and forgive him. Find some positive things to tell him about himself.

Then both of you should walk away from the discipline session as if the offense never happened.

Stay consistent. Every time your child doesn't obey you the *first time* you tell him to do something, discipline him.

If he disobeys in the same area more than once, treat the offense as though it were the first time it happened. Don't bring up past mistakes to your child's memory or give in to the temptation to say, "Why are you doing that *again*?" He has been forgiven of his past transgressions by you and God.

Your children don't need to be reminded of their sins. The Father God doesn't do that to you. He calls you a new creature in Christ and tells you that the old things have passed away (2 Cor. 5:17). He forgets your offenses when you ask Him for forgiveness. Therefore, treat your child with the same grace.

It is the devil's strategy — not God's — to remind us of what we used to be. So when it comes to disciplining our children, we need to take care of the situation scripturally, forgive our child for the offense and then forget it.

Discipline, Not Punishment

After you spank your child, don't inflict undue punishment on him by grounding him or taking his bike away from him for a week.

If God did that to us, it wouldn't be long before we would lose most of the blessings that He has given us over the years! But *God isn't in the business of taking things away from people.*

No, why don't we just do what God says to do in His Word regarding child discipline? Then after their spanking, our children can go on in freedom and forgiveness without looking back!

Of course, it's different when your children's misuse of a particular privilege (such as talking on the telephone or driving the family car) is causing a problem. In that case, you might have to restrict your child's use of the privilege for a time.

For example, there came a time after my sons reached the age of puberty that the phone just rang and rang and rang — and it was hardly ever for me! Sometimes the phone rang after the boys were in bed, and it would be some girl wanting to talk to one of them. I would say, "Too late, sweetheart, he's in bed, and he isn't coming to the phone." Otherwise, my son would get on the telephone and talk into the wee hours of the night!

Dea and I put a "fence" around the boys' telephone time. For instance, we would tell them, "You can talk to each person for no more than fifteen minutes." We had to do that for our own survival!

Remember, this was before the days of the "call waiting" feature on the telephone. I might be in Chicago trying to call home to say my flight would be late so Dea wouldn't drive to the airport and wait two hours for me in the dark. Meanwhile, I had three sons who, left to themselves, would tie up the phone all evening talking to their friends!

So if one of our sons abused his telephone privileges, we just didn't allow him to use the telephone for a while. But that's different than taking away his telephone privileges because of disobedience in another area. I just don't see that method of discipline in the Word.

God is a *giver* of all good gifts — not Someone who *takes good gifts away*! He ordained the rod as the mode of discipline, and He considers the rod adequate to do the job of training your child to obey.

So institute godly discipline in your home — but do it God's way. You will soon find out that His way works!

GUIDELINES FOR TRAINING CHILDREN

Training up your children in the way they should go involves a lot more than just disciplining them. Every step of the way, there are obstacles to avoid and biblical values to instill. Here are a few guidelines to help you raise godly children who will grow up to influence this world for God.

The Importance of a Child's Name

God is concerned what you name your children. He said this in Isaiah 49:1:

> **Listen, O isles, unto me; and hearken, ye people, from far; The Lord hath called me from the womb;** *from the bowels of my mother hath he made mention of my name.*

It is very important what you name your children, because every time you call them by their name, you are confessing what that name means over them. Therefore, I believe you should find out what a name means before you decide to give it to your unborn child.

If you conducted a word study of proper names in the Bible, you would find out that some of the "old meanies" in the Bible turned out to be exactly what their name means. They lived up to the name that was spoken over them all the days of their lives. In 1 Samuel 25:3, it speaks of Nabal acting churlish to David. Nabal's name means "foolish." His wife Abigail in verse 25 said of Nabal, **...for as his name is, so is he.**

We find an example of God naming a person for a specific reason in Luke 1 when the angel told Zacharias to name his son John. Later, when Zacharias announced what his baby's name would be, his friends were astonished.

You see, in the Jewish culture, names were passed down from generation to generation, and John wasn't a name in Zacharias' family. But the name John means "Jehovah gives," and that was the name that fit John's divine purpose and calling on this earth: to herald the coming of God's greatest gift — His Son.

So don't underestimate the importance of a name. Receive wisdom from God regarding what to name your baby.

Lay Up an Inheritance for Your Children

Also, don't put off planning for your children's financial future. Proverbs 13:22 says, **A good man leaveth an inheritance to his children's children.**

For example, I grew up on the family ranch, and when I entered the fourth grade, I found out that Dad had been busy laying up an inheritance for me since I was born. It was something he did for each of his children, and it turned out to be a great blessing to us.

When each of us was born, Dad gave us a cow. We didn't know that the cow was ours until we grew older. But through the years, every time our cow gave birth to a bull calf, Dad had it made into a steer and later sold it. If the cow gave birth to a heifer, Dad kept the calf so it could become another of our own cows. By the time we entered high school, each of us children owned a herd. In addition, Dad and Mom gave each of us five acres of wheat.

Many times parents dream about doing something like that for their children, but they never start the process. They think, *I'd like to lay something aside for the children's future, but we just can't afford it right now.* But Mom and Dad didn't create a financial hardship for themselves when they laid up that inheritance for their children, because they did it a little at a time.

Lester Sumrall, one of the greatest ministers of our day, understood the importance of laying up an inheritance for his children. When each of his sons were born, Lester would take five hundred dollars and buy stock in a certain company. By the time the boys turned sixteen, there was enough money in their accounts to buy each of them a new car. All it took for Lester's sons to be blessed like this was a little forethought and planning for the future on their father's part.

You have to plan ahead if you are going to lay up an inheritance for your children. Even if you don't have much when you begin, with wise management that small amount can multiply to bless your child when he is older.

Teach Financial Responsibility

It is a good idea to give your children a weekly allowance, even if it is only a dollar or two a week for things done around the house. You can use that allowance to teach them financial responsibility.

Whatever you do, teach them to tithe first. Have them take that tithe to church and put it in the offering plate themselves. Teach them the difference between a tithe and offering, and encourage them to give offerings as well. Then let them receive their own receipt from the church at the end of the year. This will help establish a sense of responsibility in your children to give of their tithes and offerings to their local church.

Dea and I required our sons to tithe as long as they lived in our house. And they tithed into the local church, not into our ministry. Once they moved out, they had to make the decision to tithe for themselves.

Know Your Child's Friends

People affect our lives, both for the good and for the bad. Therefore, make an effort to know your children's friends.

Until you know what kind of home those friends come from, have them come over to your house to play with your child. That way you can oversee what is going on and get acquainted with your child's playmates.

Once you know what type of household a friend comes from, you can decide whether or not you want to allow your child to play over at his house. If it is a good, moral household where peace reigns and godly values are taught, then feel free to allow your child to go over to play and perhaps even to spend the night. (Children love those overnighters!) But if worldly values are taught and practiced in the home, don't allow your child to spend his time there.

Guide Your Child's Taste in Music

What do you do when your child wants to listen to secular music? Well, I can tell you what I did with my sons. I didn't allow secular music in the home. If I heard one of the boys listening to secular music on the radio, I would go in his room and tell him, "Either change stations or turn off the radio."

Sometimes I would ask to borrow some of my sons' music tapes and then listen to them in my office. I may have not been wild about the beat of the music, but as long as the lyrics were all right, I didn't have a problem with it. In fact, I learned to like some of the boys' contemporary Christian music better than I liked the old traditional songs!

What always helped us in this area of music was the fact that we kept our children involved in the church and in the things of God. This helped them stay sensitive to the Holy Spirit throughout their teenage years. In fact, there were times that they threw away some of their music tapes — even tapes of supposedly Christian rock groups — because the music bothered their conscience. We never had to say a word to them.

For example, every year the entire family went to a ministerial convention for a week. The boys always took their satchel full of music tapes with them, and they would sit in the back seat listening to their music with their portable tape decks and headphones. Meanwhile, Dea and I would sit in front listening to our "old fogy" Christian music through the car tape deck. The Sturgeon family would have four types of music coming forth in the car at one time!

One year on our way home from the convention, I notice that Shane's music satchel looked emptier than it had when we arrived. "Shane," I asked, "did you give away a bunch of your tapes while we were at the convention?"

"No," Shane replied, "I threw them away."

"Oh, really?" I said. "I didn't know you had any tapes that needed to be thrown away."

"I didn't know either," Shane said, "but I just didn't feel right inside when I listened to some of the tapes, so I threw them away."

You see, the Spirit of God can do much more in the heart of your child than you can. So when you recognize something in your child's life that needs to be addressed but you aren't sure how to deal with it, pray in the Spirit about it for a few days before you do anything. Hear from God so you can deal with the situation in a way your child can accept. And sometimes the Holy Spirit will take care of it by changing your child's heart before you have a chance to do anything but pray!

Believe God for Your Children's Mates

Getting married is a lifetime proposition, so don't wait until your child is actively dating before you start believing God for the right mate for him.

As our sons were growing up and we learned more about the Word, Dea and I decided to believe God for our sons' mates. At the time, our oldest son was nine, our middle son was six, and our youngest son was three years old.

This is the prayer of consecration we prayed: "Lord, if our boys decide to marry, then we thank You *now* when they are nine, six, and three that You are preparing a bride for each one of them."

Of course, we knew that there are millions of young girls in this world who are saved, filled with the Holy Spirit and walking with the Lord and therefore could qualify as future wives for our sons. But we also knew that each of our boys would fall in love with and marry just one girl. Those three special girls were the ones we were believing God to prepare as mates for our three sons.

The years passed, and there came a time when God supernaturally put our three sons together with their future wives. At the time, Dea and I couldn't see the process working the way we had figured out in our minds it should work. But we just put our faith and trust in God, and today we are *very* satisfied with our new daughters — and so are our sons!

Believing for your children's mates works, and not just for the Sturgeons either!

The Value of Christian Schools

Have you ever stopped to think about how much opportunity your child's school has to influence him? Do you realize the school has your child more waking hours than you do for nine months of every year, from the time he is five until he leaves home to live on his own?

As a parent, it is important that you be involved in your child's school. If you are involved in it, you will have an idea of what is going on there. You will also have a say in what the school teaches your child.

Public schools today generally reflect the world and its values. Those values are often transmitted to your children through classroom lectures and discussion and through your children's peers.

Because school has such a tremendous influence on your child, you should continually intercede for your child's school, its policies and its staff. Believe God to put His people on the school staff — *expect* Him to do it.

For Christian parents whose children attend public school, it is vitally important for them to do whatever they can to make the school's influence a positive factor in their children's lives. But, thank God, there is an even better solution!

In these last days, God is raising up Christian educators who are founding Christian schools because of their desire to minister full time to children. Can you imagine what kind of impact can be made on this world by children who are raised in Christian homes and taught Christian precepts daily in a Christian school? Can you imagine the effect on children who are taught daily throughout their school-age years *never to doubt God's Word*?

In the fall of 1976, the church where Dea and I pastored began the Bread of Life Christian School, the same school I mentioned earlier. The results of the first school year convinced me that no Christian child should be forced into a public school situation if at all possible.

Too often we send vulnerable children off into a breeding ground of all the world vices, expecting them to singlehandedly clean up their environment. We look to the children to stand firmly against the persecution of their classmates and to lead all the mockers to Jesus Christ.

The truth is, we are sending our children to do what most adults *won't* do!

How much better it is to send your child to a Christian school where he has the freedom to develop his faith! Then instead of being a humiliated, embarrassed, futile Christian martyr at the age of ten, he can go out into the world to be a successful witness for Christ when he is older and has a more thorough understanding of the Word.

And don't worry about the absence of godly influences on the other children in public school if you choose to not put your child in a Christian school. The Holy Spirit has a way of bringing the truth to hungry children. For instance, although my boys stopped attending public school, they had many opportunities as they grew up to witness to their neighborhood friends and to lead several of them to Jesus.

By sending your children to a Christian school, you aren't isolating them from the world. Instead, you are *equipping them* with the power and ability to be successful Christian people in this world.

Most youth ministers will admit that Sunday school and youth group meetings aren't sufficient to turn a child into God's servant any more than one or two meals a week will develop a strong body. *Everyone needs a steady diet of God's Word to grow spiritually.* A good Christian school will help provide that healthy spiritual diet.

We looked at our Christian school as a valuable opportunity to direct children in the way they should go. We began the year with a varied group of children. Some had parents in the ministry; others were from broken homes. Some were saved and Spirit-filled; others were actually antagonistic toward spiritual teachings. Some parents had been praying for a Christian school; others brought their children to our school because the public school had kicked them out.

We treated all the students the same: with large doses of the Word, lots of love and strong applications of the paddle as needed. And we watched God change lives and mold children into imitators of Christ Jesus.

For example, we accepted a fifteen-year-old girl as a student who had been kicked out of the public school and was headed to a detention center. The only A this girl had ever made in all of her years in school was in her physical education class. But in her first nine weeks in our Christian school, this girl had the highest grade average of anyone in her class. And at the end of the school year, she had the highest grade average of anyone in the entire school!

During that school year, this fifteen-year-old was saved and filled with the Holy Spirit. Today her husband and children are all saved and Spirit-filled, and all of her children have attended Christian school.

Our students learned the power of prayer as we gathered together to agree in the name of Jesus for some particular need to be met. The students believed God successfully for material blessings for themselves and for others. They also saw God heal their own bodies, their sick friends and even their injured pets.

For example, one day one of the students — a little boy who was a leader among his friends — stayed home sick. The other five- and six-year-olds missed him, so they prayed for his healing. An hour later, a happy, healed boy appeared at the classroom door!

Children are eager to act on the Word. They only need to be taught how to do it.

Our staff taught the children not only that God heals, but that the believer can walk in divine health. I told the students at the beginning of the school year, "Now, I know we have to satisfy the laws of Oklahoma, but I'll tell you what — if you happen to wake up one morning feeling sick, come on to school anyway. We'll put you in the prayer room with the intercessor who prays in there every hour the school is open. She will lay hands on you and pray, and God will heal you! You don't want to miss school because of sickness and disease!"

Then I carried into the Christian school the same principle I used to reward my own children for being well. I told the students, "Believe God's Word to walk in divine health every day. And as you do, there will come a day when I'm going to let you all go home and have a day off because you've stayed *well*!"

Our students followed my counsel and believed God's Word. There were times when one of the students had to go to the prayer room so the intercessor on duty could lay hands on him and pray for him to receive healing. But it was always amazing to watch. After being in the prayer room for one or two hours, the once-sick student would just go back to class and finish his schoolwork as if he had never missed any school!

At the end of the first nine weeks, I told the students, "Not one of you has missed a single day of school because of sickness in these first nine weeks! So next Friday, I want you all to stay home. Tell your parents now if you want to go somewhere special, because you're going to have a three-day weekend. You've earned it!"

At the end of the next nine weeks, I went around giving those who had stayed well the entire second nine weeks another day off. But when I told one little boy, "You get to take the day off next Friday," he started crying!

The boy asked, "Do I have to?"

Surprised, I said, "Why, no, you don't have to. But don't you want to?"

"No!" he replied. "If I stayed home, I wouldn't be with my friends."

And do you know what? Not one child in our Christian school that year chose to take any more days off, even when he or she had earned it by staying well. The students loved school that much!

What an opportunity a Christian school has to mold young characters and to point children to the Way — Jesus!

Your children deserve an opportunity to become established firmly on the Word of God before they have to face the doubt and unbelief of this present world. A good Christian school affords them that opportunity.

In this chapter, I have just shared some simple guidelines to help you along the way as you train your children according to God's Word. None of these guidelines are formulas to memorize or strict rules to keep. But they do contain important principles from the Word that, when applied to your family, can help start a revival of godliness in your home!

PORTRAIT OF A CHRISTIAN HOME: ATTENTION, DAD!

In August 1982 while ministering near Chicago, Illinois, I was reading Psalms 127 and 128 in preparation for my message on the home and family. All of a sudden the Lord began to open up these two chapters of the Bible in a way I had never seen before.

> **Except the Lord build the house, they labour in vain that build it: except the Lord keep the city, the watchman waketh but in vain. It is vain for you to rise up early, to sit up late, to eat the bread of sorrows: for so he giveth his beloved sleep.**
>
> **Lo, children are an heritage of the Lord: and the fruit of the womb is his reward. As arrows are in the hand of a mighty man; so are children of the youth. Happy is the man that hath his quiver full of them: they shall not be ashamed, but they shall speak with the enemies in the gate.**
>
> **Psalm 127:1-5**
>
> **Blessed is every one that feareth the Lord; that walketh in his ways. For thou shalt eat the labour of thine hands: happy shalt thou be, and it shall be well with thee.**
>
> **Thy wife shall be as a fruitful vine by the sides of thine house: thy children like olive plants round about thy table. Behold, that thus shall the man be blessed that feareth the Lord.**

The Lord shall bless thee out of Zion: and thou shalt see the good of Jerusalem all the days of thy life. Yea, thou shalt see thy children's children, and peace upon Israel.

Psalm 128:1-6

As I read these two chapters, the Lord spoke to my spirit, saying, "Son, in Psalms 127 and 128, I paint you a portrait of the Christian home. Verse by verse, I put different colors on the canvas. I want to show you what a Christian family ought to be like so you can visualize it from now until the time you come to be with Me."

I don't know about you, but it helps me learn a concept when I can visualize it. That's especially true when I study God's Word. I like to look through the eyes of my spirit to see what is really going on in the passage of Scripture I am studying.

That's why I really like the Lord to paint me a picture when He is teaching me something. It gives me the opportunity to do the same thing I would do with a painting in a museum: I look at it from all sides to see its many facets and dimensions.

So many of us visualized what we thought life would be like once we were married. But soon after the wedding ceremony, we were disappointed because we had painted an unrealistic picture in our minds.

The only place you will find an accurate portrait of the Christian family is in God's Word. He wants you to be able to see through the eyes of your spirit the Christian home as He designed it to be. He wants to paint you a picture of the way your family can and should be.

Father: God Is Speaking to *You*

In these two psalms we just read, God is speaking expressly to the husband and father of the home. God is talking to the man about his children and his wife.

God is specifically speaking to someone whom He desires to be the priest in the family — the spiritual head, *not* a spiritual wimp! He is talking to someone in that Christian home who will spend time on his knees seeking the Lord to find out what direction his family is supposed to be going.

Man of the home, you need to discern the direction your family should be going — not with the mind of the flesh, but in the realm of the Spirit. Then you need to do everything you possibly can as a godly father and husband to help get your family into position to follow God's plan. Speak God's will for your family into existence by faith. Start using God's words over your children and your wife.

The Man as the Developer of the Household

God wants us as fathers to know the basic direction in life that our children should be going. He wants us to be developers — developing our children's gifts and guiding them in the right direction so they can walk in God's best for their lives.

In the natural, a developer is someone who looks at a seemingly worthless piece of land and sees the high-rise building, the condominiums or the beautiful homes that can be built there. A developer can see things that other people don't see; he can develop a piece of land that no one else wants and make it something that *everyone* wants! Then people pay a pretty price for it, and the developer becomes rich.

Well, the way you become rich in blessings as a husband and a father is to hear from the Father God regarding how to develop your household.

You see, God wants men to take their position as the spiritual leader in the home. He isn't against women, but His divine order in the home places the man in the leadership position.

Thank God, the church is beginning to see almost as many men as women in the local congregations. (And thank God, too, for all the

135

women who carried the torch of spiritual leadership before many of the men ever showed up!)

The man who doesn't take his rightful place as the spiritual leader in the home is the destroyer, not the developer, of his family. If he refuses to be the godly leader he is supposed to be, the wife must take his place as spiritual head of the family. But she will never be able to fulfill that role to the extent God intended the man to do it. Therefore, when the husband fails to fulfill his God-ordained responsibility, the family suffers.

The Highest Form of Masculinity

I believe that the most masculine men in the world are those who are truly spiritual. Men will never receive the respect they desire until they become spiritual men.

But what does it mean to be a spiritual man? Well, the best Example to learn from is Jesus. When Jesus walked the earth, He certainly was *not* a wimp. He was a man's Man. I believe when He walked by, just His physique caused people to turn and look. They had just seen the Lamb of God walk by, perfect in spirit, soul and body.

The highest form of masculinity a man can ever attain is to be like Jesus. The greatest compliment any man could ever receive from his children is for them to say, "You know, Daddy, Jesus reminds me of you." And the highest compliment a man could ever receive from his wife is for her to look at him and say, "Sweetheart, the more I know about Jesus, the more I realize that you're becoming like Him."

That quality is something to really cherish and hang on to. That's something you can build on in your life, because pride can't enter in. It is a humbling thing to have someone tell you, "You remind me of Jesus."

But to be like Jesus, you have to know His Word. And if you are going to know His Word, you have to read it. It has to be something you are consumed with. You can't spend all of your time reading *Time* magazine or USA *Today*.

There isn't anything wrong with reading the news, but it shouldn't be the first thing you pick up to read in the morning. You ought to pick up the Word of God and see what God has to say about today!

Father, Spend Time With Your Children

As the husband and father, you have a ministry above all else to your family. It's supposed to be a joyful ministry. It is certainly a ministry that God wants to flourish.

But to fulfill that ministry, it is important that you get your priorities straight. No matter how busy your life is, you have to set aside time to spend with your wife and children. Don't wait until your children have grown up and left home to look back and wish you had enjoyed them more.

For instance, I know pastors who spend a lot more time with their churches than they spend with their families. God forbid that a pastor's family go down the tubes because he spends all of his time counseling Sister Sandpaper!

Yes, fathers, you need to be a provider for your family, and that does keep you busy. But God will help you arrange your plans so you can take time off to be with your family.

I can use my own life as an example of that. At one time I was traveling in the ministry more than I should. One day on my way back to Oklahoma from some meetings in Florida, I was feeling sorry for myself, so I "bellyached" to God about it. I told Him, "Lord, I miss my family and my home. I'm out on the road for such long periods at a time because of these long meetings!"

Then the Lord spoke to my spirit very plainly, saying, "Who arranges those meetings?"

I replied, "Well, God, I believe You do. You open the door of opportunity."

"I open the doors," the Lord said, "but who makes the schedule?"

"Well, I do," I answered.

"Well, then, since you're the one who makes your schedule, you're the one who will have to change it. You say that you don't like being out on the road away from your family for twenty-plus days at a time?"

"No, I don't," I said.

"Then change it."

"What do I change it to?" I asked.

"Nine days," He said, "and those nine days should include travel time."

"But, Lord," I protested. "when I arrive in a certain area to preach in one church, other pastors want me to visit their churches too. One opportunity leads to another, and it all takes longer than nine days!"

"The meeting you originally scheduled that took you to that city in the first place is the one I called you to hold. The other pastors try to add their churches to your list because they think that that they can't afford you otherwise. They're just trying to save money.

"So minister only to the people who schedule you, and then go back to be with your family. If the other pastors want you, let them bring you back to their city themselves.

"You see," the Lord explained to me, "you should be home *more* than you are out on the road. You can't go out and teach on the Christian home and family to the body of Christ and not be a good example of a husband and a father in your own home."

Now that was a rhema word to me right when I needed it! So I rearranged my schedule according to the Lord's instructions and got my family back at the top of my priority list where they belonged, right below my relationship with God.

Ever since I was born again and Spirit-filled, I understood the importance of spending quality time with my sons. While they were in grade school, I started setting aside nine specific days each year to go play with them, more often than not at the family ranch. Now that my sons are grown, we still set aside those same nine days to go down to the ranch to camp out, hunt and have fun together.

There was a time when all four of us could fit in a pup tent. But as the boys grew bigger, it became harder to do that. (Now I can barely fit in one all by myself!) We laughed ourselves silly at night trying to find a way for all of us to lay down.

We would finally figure out where each boy should lay his head and settle ourselves down to sleep. Then when everything had been quiet for a while, one of the boys would say, "I have to go to the bathroom" — and we'd start laughing all over again!

Those are some of the good memories the boys and I still cherish today of our times together when they were growing up. Today I am a grandfather myself, but as I walk through the family ranch, fond memories of times spent with my own father and grandfather still warm my heart.

I look over and see a tree where my father, my grandfather and I spotted a bobcat one day as we passed by. Or I walk past what we called the "bridal wreath tree," where my dad and I would quietly sit together to watch deer walk by on a nearby path.

I have such good memories of those days. My father and grandfather gave me a precious heritage by spending those many hours with me when I was a boy.

It is just good to enjoy special times together with your family. But if you allow yourself to become too busy with work or other outside activities, you miss out on making those precious memories with your children and your wife.

Some men will plan to do something fun with their family for the day. But then their mother, father, aunt or buddy from work will call to ask for help, and the men drop everything to make room for the new demands on their time.

No, your family should take precedence. If you told your family you would take them fishing on Saturday, that takes precedence over anything else, because you put your word out. If you said you were going to do that with your family, you need to do it whether it rains, snows or sleets. Do it because you told them you would.

That's important. Children respect a mother and father who live up to their word — and God does too!

Always Make Room for Your Children

The Bible says we can call God "Abba, Father" (Rom. 8:15). In our vernacular, the word "abba" can be translated "papa" or "daddy." The heart cry of a mature son is to call the father whom he loves by the intimate name "Daddy" or "Papa."

It is easy for me to have a close, personal relationship with my Papa God because when I was growing up, my daddy and I were as close as any son and father I have ever seen. Daddy died when he was fifty-four years old, but I thank God for all my memories of the short years I had with him.

If I were to put into one statement the relationship I shared with my father, it would be this: "Daddy always made room for me." There was always a place for me with my dad.

The Father God is that way too. He says to you, "Your big Brother Jesus is seated at My right hand. And because My Son shed His blood for you, I'm sitting in the throne room just waiting for you to come up into the heavenlies to sit on My lap and let Me love you."

So if you ever feel alone, just go up to the throne room of God and sit down on Papa's lap. Let Him put His arms around you as you minister to Him in praise and worship. Just get your eyes completely off the things of this world and go boldly to your Papa God in time of need (Heb. 4:16). He will help you out!

I learned about my heavenly Father's love for me as I grew up experiencing my daddy's love. For instance, I will never forget the time we bought our very first *new* tractor. That new tractor had an electric starter on it. That was a very big deal. We didn't have to handcrank our old tractor anymore!

I was just a little boy, and I remember being so proud as I rode in my dad's old "bobtail" truck with my uncle, watching my daddy drive a *brand new* Case tractor away from that farm implement dealership. We followed Daddy the entire twenty-eight miles to the homeplace, and every time a car drove by, I wanted to roll the window down and holler, "That's my daddy! That's our brand new tractor!"

Dad parked the new tractor inside the garage where the bobtail truck generally sat. Then he and my uncle walked around the tractor, kicking the tires and looking at the nice paint job and electric starter.

After a while, Mama hollered to them, "The coffee's ready!" Well, I was just a little boy; I didn't drink coffee. So I decided to stay and look at the new tractor.

As my uncle walked out of the garage, he said to my dad, "Bud, better not leave that boy out here alone. He'll start that tractor."

"Oh, he can't start it," Dad said.

When I heard that, I thought, *Well, I'll show Daddy I can!* I thought my dad would be pleased to find out I was smart enough to start the tractor all by myself.

I had watched how my dad and uncle pulled both the spark and the throttle back just so far, and I knew where the little starter button was that had to be pushed.

So I started up that tractor, and I tell you what — my dad stopped drinking his coffee real fast! He ran out to the garage, and he did *not* look very pleased.

Daddy explained to me the seriousness of my offense. "What if you had put the tractor in gear and run it through the garage door?" he asked. Then he spanked me because I had done something I wasn't supposed to do.

After supper, Daddy went back out to the garage, and I didn't see him again before I went to bed. To this day I can remember how terrible I felt as I lay in bed, thinking about what I had done with that tractor.

It always really bothered me if I felt a strain between me and my daddy. But this time I felt even worse because all the excitement of the day had left, and I had been disciplined for something I thought my dad would be proud of me for doing. I hadn't recognized the danger involved.

The next morning I woke up thinking, *Daddy is going to hook that new tractor to the mower and start mowing our alfalfa, and now I won't get to go.* I had always gone with my dad before. He had fixed up a little seat on the fender of the old tractor, and I always sat there so I could be with him.

But after breakfast, Daddy said to me, "Come on, let's go mow hay." Unknown to me, my dad had stayed up almost all night, taking that little seat off the old tractor fender and fastening it to the new tractor. He wasn't about to take that tractor out and mow hay without his son! That's what I mean when I say my dad always made a place for me.

Daddy and I did everything together, so the first day I started first grade was a terrible day for me (there wasn't any kindergarten back then). I knew my dad was going to a livestock auction that day, and I couldn't be there. I never did learn to like grade school, even though I made satisfactory grades, and the main reason I didn't was that it separated me from my father.

But despite having to go to school, I found out Daddy and I could still be close and enjoy doing things together. He always made sure he spent a lot of time with me.

So later when I discovered I had a heavenly Father who loved me, it wasn't difficult for me to believe that, because I knew how much my earthly father loved me.

Today I can walk for hours on the ranch where I grew up and recall one memory after another of good times spent with my earthly father. And while I'm out on our land, I like to spend time with my heavenly Father as well. I like to climb one of the nearby hills where I can see for miles. I sit there for hours, praying in tongues and worshiping God.

God ministers to me as I sit there alone with Him. He gives me direction for my family; He corrects me in areas where I need to adjust. He is Papa God to me.

I have compassion for those who don't have my kind of testimony about their earthly fathers. But once a person is washed by the blood of Jesus and learns to go before the throne of God to receive help, the Father God will heal every hurt from his past. God wants to be "Abba Father" — Papa God — to every one of His children.

Our Father God always makes a place for you. He will make your Christian home a place of safety, comfort, peace and refuge. He will make your family strong. He promises to perfect that which concerns you (Ps. 138:8). Whatever is on your heart concerning your home and family, Papa God will take care of it.

So as an earthly father, spend time before your heavenly Father. Hear from Him regarding the direction your family should be going and the needs of each family member. Learn how to know the needs of your wife and your children before they ever talk to you about them.

Become the spiritual leader God always intended for you to be in the divine portrait He is painting of your home!

PORTRAIT OF A CHRISTIAN HOME: LET THE LORD BUILD THE HOUSE

Let's take a closer look at the portrait God paints of the Christian home in Psalms 127 and 128. God starts out by saying that He must be the Master Artist of that divine portrait — the Builder of your home.

Except the Lord build the house, they labour in vain that build it: except the Lord keep the city, the watchman waketh but in vain.

Psalm 127:1

If you give me a hammer, nails and a pile of wood, I will be stuck with a hammer, nails and a pile of wood. I won't know what to do with them, because I am not a carpenter. But if you give the same three items to a carpenter, he is capable of using them to build a beautiful, finished home.

In the same way, you don't know how to build a successful Christian home on your own. But if you give your family to Jesus, He can build your home into a beautiful, finished product of security, joy and happiness that brings glory to Him. Remember, He is the Author and the Finisher of your faith (Heb. 12:2). He knows how to complete the work God has begun in you and your loved ones.

It Takes the Lord To Build the House

People try all sorts of things in their search for a successful home life. Some look to psychology; others study folk lore; and others even turn to witchcraft as they try to find out how to have a happy, peaceful family. But the answer is found only in the Word, and the Word says, "It takes the Lord to build the house; otherwise, you're going to labor in vain."

Sometimes within a family, the husband and wife or the children and parents can seem to be each other's worst enemies. If that is the case in your home, you need to put your trust in God's ability to build your home into what He wants it to be. Proverbs 16:7 says, **When a man's ways please the Lord, he maketh even his enemies to be at peace with him.**

You may be believing God for your mate to come in line with the Word of God. You may think at times, *If I could just say the right thing, maybe she (or he) would change.* But you don't have to figure out what you should do or say to change your spouse. Just trust God with your mate. God won't make a mistake. When He touches a person's heart, it is forever. He knows how to build the house.

Don't labor in vain trying to build your house in your own strength. In other words, don't sweat over it! Let the power of the Holy Ghost establish a strong, godly home, whether it is in the area of disciplining your children or in your marriage relationship. And as you keep trusting God, He will set the stage for the necessary adjustments and changes to take place in your home.

How the Lord Built the Sturgeon Home

How can I be so sure of that? Well, I saw firsthand the power of God at work in the Sturgeon home after I was born again and Spirit-filled. After being an alcoholic for many years, I desperately needed the Lord to build the home I had almost destroyed with my sinful ways.

Right after I was born again, I lost everything but my wife, my three sons and Jesus. I signed away the inheritance my father had left me. We were left standing in a house that only cost us sixty-five dollars a month to rent — and we couldn't even pay the rent!

146

I watched the people pull all of our farm machinery down the driveway. We had to sell everything we had, and then they charged us for what was left over.

I was advised to file for bankruptcy, but I wanted to make sure all of my creditors were paid. I had been an alcoholic. I knew that I was suffering the consequences of serving the devil for so many years.

During those dark years before I got saved, I would spend all of my time in beer joints, bars or clubs throughout northwest Oklahoma. I was hardly ever with my family or at my home. I was always somewhere else drinking and losing all the money I had.

But I had a good wife who got right with God. And the Lord promised her that He could straighten out her household if she would trust Him.

After praying several hours a day for me for almost three months, one day my little sweetheart stood in that rented home without me hearing her and said, "God, I'll give you two weeks to get Chuck saved and filled with the Holy Spirit."

I believe God gave Dea a word of wisdom that prompted her to say that, because it was exactly fourteen days later that a Spirit-filled elderly couple drove twenty-eight miles to our home to minister God's Word to me. I believe God was actually speaking to Dea's spirit, saying, "Sweetheart, turn your husband over to Me. If you'll do that, in fourteen days he will be saved and filled with the Holy Spirit."

During that elderly couple's second visit to our home, I was saved, filled with the Holy Spirit and set free from every dirty, nasty thing I had ever done. I also saw a vision of Jesus, and He reminded me that I had made a commitment to Him when I was nine years old to preach the gospel.

All that happened at night while my three boys were asleep. The next morning at the breakfast table, Dea asked seven-year-old Mike, "Mike, do you notice a change in your daddy?"

Mike replied, "Yes, he must have gotten saved."

How did Mike know that? Because he was born again himself. (When Mike had gotten saved earlier, I had been so degenerate, I wouldn't even let him be baptized in the church or receive the Bible the church wanted to give him!)

Now it was my turn to be born again and Spirit-filled. And even though I hadn't said anything to the boys that morning, Mike knew by the Spirit that between the time he had gone to sleep the night before and the time he woke up, his dad had been born again.

Less than twenty-four hours after getting saved, I was already full of the Word. How could that be? Because my parents had made me go to church as a child, and God's Word will never return void. Even though I hadn't been born again, my spirit had soaked up that Word.

So the next morning after receiving Jesus and the baptism of the Holy Spirit, I discovered that every bit of the Word ever planted in my spirit as a boy was coming back to my remembrance. I was quoting Scripture to Dea that I had never memorized in the church of my youth. And since that day, the Sturgeon family has never been the same!

So don't ever doubt God's Word. If you are trusting in God and obeying His Word, He is working in your family. He *is* working in your home. No matter what kind of mess your home may be in, don't give up too quickly. Keep believing God to build your house into a thing of beauty and divine order.

One thing I have noticed with so-called faith people is that they give up too quickly. The way I read the Bible, we are *never* to give up!

Too often a Christian couple decides, *He's never going to change. She's never going to change. My children are never going to change. Using the rod isn't working. I don't see results.* So they give up, and they miss out on the opportunity to see God perform a miracle in their family.

I want to encourage you to *never give up*. We are on the offense, not the defense, with the devil. It's our ball; it's our bat; and Papa God is our Umpire. How can we lose? The devil may say, "Three strikes, and you're out!" But God just says, "Oh, no, you don't. My boy gets to stay up to bat until he hits a home run!"

We are *more* than conquerors! (Rom. 8:37). As more than conquerors, we can know we have won before we even fight the battle. Our part is to apply our faith in the Word of God to our families and then let God build our house.

You see, God wants you to help Him build your house, but He is the One who will ultimately do it. You won't have to struggle to establish a godly home in your own natural strength. It won't be built by the sweat of your brow. Remember, you serve a God who is El Shaddai, the God who is more than enough!

God Gives to You While You Sleep

Let's go on to Psalm 127:2, which tells us that sadness and worry shouldn't be hanging around the Christian home:

It is vain for you to rise up early, to sit up late, to eat the bread of sorrows: for so he giveth his beloved sleep.
Psalm 127:2

A more literal translation of that verse would be "He gives to His beloved while he sleeps."[1] You see, your spirit doesn't sleep. During the hours you lay in bed asleep, God can be ministering to your spirit. You can have spiritual dreams and visions in the night — and get a good night's rest at the same time!

You can train your spirit to be so in tune with God that when there are needs in your family, God by His Spirit will pray through you, building up

---

[1] Isaac Leeser, *Twenty-Four Books of the Holy Scriptures* (New York: Hebrew Publishing Co., n.d.), p. 1074.

your most holy faith even as your body sleeps. You can get in the habit of going to sleep praying in tongues and waking up still praying in tongues. You may find that praying in the Spirit becomes so much a part of you that at times you wake yourself up in the middle of the night speaking out loud in tongues.

Just go to bed with the attitude "Papa God is going to give to me while I sleep." As you do, you open your spirit to absorb from Him as your body rests.

Don't Eat the Bread of Sorrows

God is also saying in Psalm 127:2, "Stop worrying and talking about your problem all the time. When you do, you are eating the bread of sorrows, and it's vain for you to do that." So when it comes time to go to bed, just forget about the circumstances you have to deal with tomorrow. Don't talk the problem right before going to bed.

That's what a lot of mothers and fathers do in Christian homes: They rise up early and sit up late at night, talking about the problem. But God says, "It is vain, or useless, to do that."

I hear about so many husbands and wives who say to each other, "Let's wait until the children go to sleep — and then all hell is going to break loose! I'm going to tell you what I *really* think about this!" Then they stay up until 3:00 in the morning arguing about the problem.

But the Bible says, "Don't let the sun go down on your wrath" (Eph. 4:26). If the sun already went down; it isn't the time for wrath. (Not that there is *ever* a time for fleshly wrath!)

Instead of plowing into a big argument right before bedtime, just say, "Hey, Sweetheart, we can't solve this — only God can." Then kiss and make up. (Making up is always more fun anyway!)

Put your head on trouble itself and use it as a pillow. Say, "Bless God, we're going to sleep! We are casting all the cares of this family over on the Lord. There isn't anything too hard for Him!" Then pray in the Spirit and go to sleep. Let God minister to you through the night.

If you want to sit up late at night and do something, talk the answer. And as you talk the answer, you'll have peace. That supernatural peace will guard your heart and mind in Christ Jesus, and you will get a good night's rest.

And when your feet hit the floor in the morning, God will speak to you and tell you what to do that day. After all, He knew you before you were ever born! All you have to do is ask, "Lord, what did You see me doing today when You planned my life before the foundations of the earth?" God will let you know what to do. You will walk on in peace, knowing He is on your side.

Not in Front of the Children

So make it a way of life not to talk the problem. If there are certain situations and problems that have to be discussed between you and your spouse, do it privately without the children listening in on the conversation.

You and your spouse need a place where you can go to privately discuss and pray about situations as a mother and father. I recommend that you make the master bedroom, your "love chamber," that private place. The children can be trained not to go in there unless invited, even if the door is open. And if the door is closed, they can be trained not to knock or ask you to open the door unless it is an emergency.

Also, it is important for us as parents to refrain from talking negatively about relatives or anyone else in front of the children. When we talk about the problems we face with other people in front of our children, the children may start to form wrong attitudes against the particular people we are talking about. And, of course, children are very open, and they will sometimes talk about matters they have heard that don't need to be shared with anyone else.

We should never put undue responsibility on a child by saying, "Now, you aren't to tell anyone what Mama and Daddy said." If we have something that shouldn't be known by others outside the home, then we should keep it unknown to our children as well.

And for those of us in the ministry, we need to understand that it is unfair for us to talk about the problems of the church all the time over meals, during family outings and vacations, and so forth. As Rev. Kenneth E. Hagin says (from whom I have learned so much over the years), "Your children ought to think that everyone in the church is a saint."

After all, in a child's mind, if everyone is serving God, why should there be a problem? Children just aren't mature enough yet to sort all that out.

Your Children: A Heritage of the Lord

As we read Psalm 127:3, we discover the way God paints children into His portrait of the Christian home:

> **Lo, children are an heritage of the Lord: and the fruit of the womb is his reward.**
>
> **Psalm 127:3**

Perhaps you are pregnant with a child you didn't plan for. Or perhaps your pregnancy didn't come along in the timing you had planned. No matter what, you are still to receive your child as a blessing of the Lord.

The Bible calls little children *a heritage of the Lord*. The literal translation of the Hebrew word *heritage* means "prized possessions." Children are prized possessions — not yours, but the Lord's. The fruit of the womb is His reward or compensation (v. 3).

God is saying to us as Christian parents, "I give your children to you to be blessings in your life. My reward for that gift — what you can give back to Me in repayment — is to raise your children in the admonition of the Lord." You see, God wants us to leave on this earth godly seed — children who know how to live by faith.

When parents find out they are going to have another child, they sometimes joke about it, saying, "I need another child like I need a hole in my head." But that's a prized possession of the Lord they are talking about!

The fruit of the womb is the Lord's reward upon conception. That's why abortion is murder. God is able to see into the loins of a man and know his children before they are even conceived.

For instance, the angel told John the Baptist's daddy, "Your wife Elizabeth shall bear thee a son" (Luke 1:13). God could see that child, His prized possession, in the loins of his daddy before he was ever conceived in his mother's womb.

What do people do in the secular world with a prized possession? They cherish it; they may even build a big museum to house it. They put it behind glass and hire a guard to protect it. They watch that prized possession like a hawk because it is one of a kind.

Well, how much more should we cherish our children, who are the prized possessions of the Lord? How much more interested should we be in meeting our children's needs than in acquiring a bunch of material possessions in pursuit of "the good life"?

Dea and I have the only Michael Allen Sturgeon, the only Brian Charles Sturgeon, the only Bud Shane Sturgeon there is; they are each one of a kind. They are prized possessions, but they aren't ours — they belong to the Lord. God gave each of them to us, and then He said, "Do you want to recompense Me? Just raise these children to be godly, and then trust Me to take care of them."

It is so important to make sure that your children are in church every Sunday and that they are taught the Word in their home. Why? Because they aren't really yours; they are the Lord's, and He wants holy seed. If Jesus tarries and we all die and go home to be with the Lord, God wants us to leave behind a heritage of godly children to carry on the work of His kingdom.

Your Children: Weapons of Defense

In God's eyes, children are not only prized possessions; they are weapons of defense that He has placed in your hand.

As arrows are in the hand of a mighty man; so are children of thy youth. Happy is the man that hath his quiver full of them: they shall not be ashamed, but they shall speak with the enemies in the gate.

Psalm 127:4-5

Your children are as arrows to you. They aren't for the *death* of you; they are for the *life* of you. They are weapons of defense *for* you, not *against* you. And the Bible says, **Happy is the man that hath his quiver full of them!**

How many happy parents do we see today? Any parent who is saved and filled with the Spirit ought to be happy, full of joy and strengthened by the Lord — especially if they have a quiverful of children!

Well, what is a quiverful? Just as many children as you and your spouse want to have. I believe that God gives you as parents enough sense to pray and determine before God how many children you want to have and then to give birth to just that number.

If you want to have thirteen children, you can have thirteen. If you want to adopt four more children, you can adopt four more. If you want to be the foster parent of five more children on top of that, go ahead and do it!

It isn't anyone else's business. It doesn't even make any difference whether or not Grandma and Grandpa want to buy extra gifts for all those children at Christmas! If you and your spouse know you can handle the extra responsibility, that's all that matters.

Several years ago, I preached at a little church in Louisiana that owned a small school bus. The next time I preached at the church, the bus was gone. "What did you do with that school bus?" I happened to ask a church member.

"Well, we sold it to a family."

"A family? How many children does that family have?" I asked.

"Thirteen," the man said. "And the mother and father are going to adopt a few other children as well!" (The last I heard, the couple had seventeen children in all!)

The man informed me that this family had gotten tired of driving their children back and forth to school, so they built a Christian school on their land. They also built a girls' dorm on one side of the house and a boys' dorm on the other side.

Then the man commented, "It's the strangest thing. A family that big, and they paid for the bus not only in cash, but in silver dollars!"

That shouldn't be so surprising. You see, people think that if parents have a lot of children, the financial burden will be so great that they will have to go on welfare. But that is unscriptural thinking. The Bible says that children are a *blessing* of the Lord!

Point Your Arrows in the Right Direction

Your children are to be weapons of defense *for* you. But if they aren't living in line with God's Word in your home, they become a weapon *against* you. That's why it hurts so much when you experience problems with your children.

So what do you do if your arrow has turned the wrong direction? Well, father, Psalm 127:4 calls you a mighty man. You are the priest of the family, and you are supposed to point those arrows in your hand back in the right direction — toward the glory of God and dedication to the Lord.

How do you do that? With the authority of Jesus Christ. It is just that simple. You are to pray in the Spirit, meditate on God's promises concerning your children and speak that Word over them. You are also to go ahead of them in life, making "tracks in the snow" so they can step into them and follow your example.

What do I mean by that? Well, I once saw a Christmas card with a painting of a father walking through the snow in the country, carrying a saddle over his back. Behind him was his little bitty boy, stretching his feet out as far as he could to step in his father's tracks in the snow.

We can do that for our children in life as we train them up in the way they should go. Then if a need arises when we aren't present, they will just step into our footprints and operate in their authority in Christ as we have taught them. They will step from the quiver to the bow and shoot straight toward the mark, doing whatever Dad or Mom would have done.

They will become the arsenal of defense they are supposed to be for us in our middle years and in our old age. And when we have need of someone coming to our defense, our children will probably be the first to offer help.

For instance, I have to be careful what I say around my sons. If I just casually say that I need or would like to have a particular item, they will go to great lengths to find it and buy it for me! They are my weapons of defense, and they have so much fun giving me something they know I want or need.

A Polished Shaft

In Isaiah 49:2, the coming Messiah is likened to an arrow whose shaft God polishes. But the same principle can apply to the arrows in your quiver — your children:

In the shadow of his [God's] hand hath he hid me, and made me a polished shaft; in his quiver hath he hid me.

Anyone who is an archer knows that the shaft of an arrow is extremely important when attempting to hit a target. When a shaft is polished, it can go through the elements of the earth and air with such speed, ability and power that it is much more likely to hit the exact mark at which it was aimed.

Well, God will not only make your children arrows in your quiver, but He will give them polished shafts to help them hit the mark — His perfect will for their lives.

When a man who has his quiver full of children serves God, God hides that man's quiver in His own quiver. God adds His own infinite power to the best of that father's ability to polish the shafts of his little arrows.

Your Children as Concealed Weapons

The *New International Version* puts Isaiah 49:2 this way: **He made me into a polished arrow and concealed me in his quiver.** Our children are like concealed weapons in the quiver of God.

For example, during the Persian Gulf War, many of us learned that the United States armed forces had weapons that we previously knew nothing about. We saw on television how precisely these weapons could hit the mark. Those concealed weapons ended that war quickly once they were revealed and utilized.

Well, Papa God has a quiverful of concealed weapons — namely, us! We are all concealed weapons for God. And when necessary, we can be released very quickly to hit the mark as we exercise our God-given authority to stop the work of the enemy on this earth.

So God says to us parents, "I'll tell you what. You have some concealed weapons of your own, and I have plenty of room in My quiver.

Let me hide them in My quiver. And when it's time, you can pull them out and shoot them in the direction I want them to fly."

Even after you have pulled back the bowstring and released your arrows to fly toward the mark of God's call, those children will remain weapons of defense for you throughout life. They will be your protectors.

For instance, when Dea and I need help, our boys are always there to do whatever they can. And if they can't be there, they want to be there. Their desire is to be helpful and to minister to us. Their desire is to help Mom and Dad.

Possessing the Gates of the Enemy

Also, notice that the arrows in your quiver have a job to do: **they shall speak with the enemies in the gate** (Ps. 127:5).

If your arrows have been raised in the admonition of the Lord according to the laws and principles of God's Word, they will know how to do their job. They will know how to take the Word of God and speak to their enemies at the gate. This is a part of the covenant God made with Abraham, the father of our faith:

> **That in blessing I will bless thee, and in multiply-ing I will multiply thy seed as the stars of the heaven, and as the sand which is upon the sea shore; and *thy seed shall possess the gate of his enemies.***
>
> **Genesis 22:17**

You see, there is a gate or door to each of our lives that the devil wants to come through. We may think, *The devil is coming at me from so many directions!* But actually, he is just coming in from the gate — the gates of hell.

If the enemy is beating up on our families, then one way or another, we let him in through that gate. Well, let's keep that gate closed to our homes. Let's be watchers of the gate! And when Mom and Dad aren't there to watch it, our children will do it for us — *if* we have trained them in the way they should go.

When the gate is left open for any reason and you aren't around to close it, your children will be able to tell the devil, "No, Mama and Daddy might not be here right now, but you can't touch this home! They have taught us about you, Mr. Devil, and in the name of Jesus Christ of Nazareth, we bind you and possess that gate!"

For example, several years ago Dea and I were on the road ministering, and I sensed an urgency to call home. Nineteen-year-old Mike answered the phone, and he had some sad news to tell me.

A family to whom we had ministered to in the past had been moving from Ohio to Florida when a tragedy occurred along the way. While eating at a restaurant, the couple's sixteen-year-old son, Rusty, ate a piece of steak that lodged in his throat. All attempts at unlodging the piece of steak had failed, and Rusty went on home to be with Jesus.

This couple was hurting deeply. They were far away from all their loved ones and friends, so besides calling their pastor in Ohio, they called me for prayer.

Mike said, "Daddy, they called here, and I answered the phone. They wanted you to pray for them."

I was still in shock from the news. "Well, Son," I said, "give me their phone number, and I'll call them."

"There isn't any need to do that, Daddy," Mike said.

"Why not, Son?"

"Because when they said that they wanted you to pray with them, I told them you weren't here. Then I told them that I could pray with them for you. I went ahead and did that, and then I asked, 'Now, do you want Dad to call you?' But they said, 'No, that's all right. We have peace in our hearts now that you prayed for us. We appreciate that so much.'"

159

What happened in this situation? When someone asked me to do something defensively in the Spirit for them and I wasn't there to do it, my arrow stood in my place! He did what he knew his daddy would do.

Mike spoke to the enemy at the gate, telling the devil, "No, you aren't going to bother this family anymore. Rusty is with the Lord, and in the name of Jesus, you aren't going to load his parents down with guilt and condemnation because of what happened!" Then Mike sent them on the family on their way in peace.

How did Mike know what to do in that difficult situation? He had been taught over the years how to use his faith.

As sad as I was over the news I had just heard, I felt a real joy inside after I hung up the telephone. I thought, *Mike has really been listening all these years!* My arrow of defense had stood in my place.

The Ministry of a Mother

Now let's let Psalm 128 paint another part of God's portrait of the Christian home.

> **Blessed is every one that feareth the Lord; that walketh in his ways. For thou shalt eat the labour of thine hands: happy shalt thou be, and it shall be well with thee.**
> **Thy wife shall be as a fruitful vine by the sides of thine house: thy children like olive plants round about thy table. Behold, that thus shall the man be blessed that feareth the Lord.**
> **Psalm 128:1-4**

In this divine portrait of the Christian family, God describes the mother as **a fruitful vine by the sides of thine house.**

I know what that verse is talking about. When I was a little boy growing up on the ranch, my mama decided to start a bunch of ivy growing on the north side of the house. She had seen a house where ivy covered an entire wall, and she liked the way it looked.

Mama was adamant about making sure her ivy survived — but between our guinea hens, chickens, geese, ducks, dogs, cats and pet deer, those little ivy shoots almost didn't make it. Not only that, but my two sisters and I often chased each other around the north side of the house.

But all three of us children and every one of our animals knew that if we started tromping around in that ivy, Mama would be after us, yelling, "You stay away from my ivy!"

Over the years, that ivy vine finally got ahead of the deer and the children and the guineas and the dogs until it absolutely covered the north side of the house.

Then after my father passed away, my mother decided she was going to paint the house. She called a painter to come and give her an estimate of the cost. When the painter walked around to the north side of the house, he almost fell over from shock.

"Mrs. Sturgeon," he said, "I *can't* paint this side of the house with that vine there! And it's so deeply rooted into the side of your house that if I were to tear the vine off, I would also be tearing off your house's siding!"

That is a very good picture of what the mama is to the Christian home. As **a fruitful vine by the sides of thine house,** the mother's main ministry is deeply rooted into the home. Her deepest instinct and her highest calling is to be a mama.

Pulling a mother out of her home often tears on her heart the way pulling out my mama's vine would have torn off the house's siding. It pulls at a mother when she has to take her children to a daycare center or a baby sitter. In her heart, she wants to be home with her children.

But over the years, the tendency in society has been to convince the mother that she should work outside of the home so she can bring in a second check to pay the bills and buy the "extras" that go with a higher standard of life. That tendency has gradually been pulling the Christian family apart.

Before our sons were born, Dea had a job at a local hospital, working until just hours before our first son, Mike, was born. But throughout our boys' upbringing, Dea was home with them. And if she traveled with me to minister, we had a born-again, Spirit-filled couple who lived with them while we were gone. To the boys, that couple was "Mom and Dad Number Two."

Many times our boys traveled with us in the ministry. When they were on the road with us, we home schooled them. We always felt it was necessary to keep our family together as much as we possibly could. We have never regretted our efforts to do that.

If you are a working mother, don't get under condemnation because of what I am saying here. I am not giving you chapter and verse that states, "Thou shalt not work outside the home." However, I *am* saying that while the children are being raised, your main ministry as a mother is in the home.

And I have a message to the man of the house: If Jesus provides for His bride, I believe we ought to provide for ours!

You may say, "Well, we can't afford to have my wife stop working." Well, then, use your faith in this matter! Believe God to make a way for your wife to quit her job if she wants to and come home to be with the children. After all, being a mama is a full-time job in itself!

Feed the Word Around the Table

Psalm 128:3 also likens your children to **olive plants round about thy table.**

If you study the subject of olive trees, you will find out that this tree lives longer than many other kinds of trees. Therefore, the olive tree stands for longevity of life.[1]

Your children have the potential of living long, fruitful lives. God talks to children in Ephesians 6:1-3. He tells them, "If you will obey your parents, you will live long on this earth."

On the other hand, if children refuse to obey their mother and father, they may very well *not* live long on this earth. They open themselves up to meeting a tragic end to a short life. That just should not be!

So make it a practice to train your little olive saplings while they are sitting around the table. Mealtime is the best time to feed your children the Word. While the family shares physical food, you can be ministering spiritual food to them.

How do you do that? First, pray over every meal, and teach your children how to pray. Also, take time to read the Word at every meal. Share times of talking about the Word together as a family. Don't just talk about the problems of the day or what is on the news. Make sure mealtime is a precious time of building family memories, where your olive plants learn to grow strong in the Lord and live long on the earth.

You Will See Your Children's Children

Psalm 128 ends with a promise of blessing and long life for the parents who have established a godly home:

The Lord shall bless thee out of Zion: and thou shalt see the good of Jerusalem all the days of thy life. Yea, thou shalt see thy children's children, and peace upon Israel.

Psalm 128:5-6

---

[1] Encyclopedia Americana, Deluxe Library Edition, Vol. 20 (Grolier, Inc., 1992), p. 713.

I have told the devil many times that I am not going to leave this world because of sickness and disease. Sickness isn't going to force me out of my body and cause me to leave this earthly life before it is my time to die.

When will it be my time to die? When I am satisfied that I am ready to leave this earthly life.

The Bible says that it is appointed unto every man once to die (Heb. 9:27). Well, unless the rapture of the church comes first, I am going to make my appointment with physical death. My appointment to leave earth is after I see my children's children's children's children!

That will probably put me at about one hundred and fifteen years old. If Jesus tarries, I'm staying here till then, and I am going to live a healthy, full life while I am here! And if you don't believe it, just wait and see.

You see, I am enjoying my life with my family too much to want to leave any sooner than that. I am so blessed to have my sweetheart. I am so blessed with my sons, my "daughter-in-loves" and my grandson. And I am speaking "more babies!" over my married sons all the time. I am looking forward to seeing my children's children's children's children!

Grandparenting 101

A good man leaveth an inheritance to his children's children: and the wealth of the sinner is laid up for the just.

Proverbs 13:22

I have been young, and now am old; yet I have not seen the righteous forsaken, nor his seed begging bread. He is ever merciful, and lendeth; and his seed is blessed.

Psalm 37: 25-26

It seems to me parenting really shows itself strong when "grand" is added to it (grandparent). At this writing, we have three grandchildren. When our six-year-old grandson Jonathan was still in his mother's womb, God gave me a dream about him. I saw him as a boy, and I was holding him in my arms while talking to another man. When I finished talking to the man, Jonathan, just a baby, turned and said the very same thing to the man. Several months later through another brother in the Lord I received the interpretation of that dream: The reason Jonathan is saying the same thing to that man is that he will be a minister of God just like you.

We held that in our hearts until this school year when Jonathan started telling others that he was going to be like his Papa when he grew up, a preacher. Even his classmates in Christian school call him "the preacher." I know there will still be several years to wait, but we already truly see him ministering the Word.

What I want you to see is this: As in Proverbs 13:22, we can leave all our grandchildren an inheritance. Whether it be spiritual or natural, it will be according to the Word. As grandparents, we should never interfere in any way with the raising of our grandchildren, but we should be there when asked to help. It could be in just giving advice or wisdom.

We see helping our children pay for Christian schooling as one way to help. Jonathan would not know what he knows about God and the Word without it. His parents and children's church can be so vitally assisted with Christian schooling. Many of us older ones need to see the vision of Christian schooling whether we have grandchildren or not. If you cannot give extra finances to help a Christian school, then help out at the school on a volunteer basis.

One day this spring I picked Jonathan up from his kindergarten class and brought him home with me. His Mammaw was busy so I fixed him lunch. Before eating he started praying, followed the prayer by a long silence and then said "Amen!" I asked him why he was silent. He replied, "Papa, I was giving Jesus free time."

"Free time?" I inquired.

"Yes, you should give Him free time so He can say something to you."

You can even learn from your grandchildren! Amen!

Being older is a plus. I am looking forward to growing old. If I leave here before the rapture, it will be because I want to and not because sickness and disease forced me out of my body. You see if that time comes, I'll gather all the family around and throw a party. At the close of the day I want to lay hands on them all and prophesy before leaving. Don't you know they will want to remember those last words!

My grandfather Turner awakened one day and didn't get out of bed. After much encouragement from Grandma, he still refused to get up. Grandma called her two girls, one being my mother, Pearl. They tried to get him to eat or get up but to no avail. Finally he said, "I'm going home today."

They said, "But you are home."

He proclaimed, "No I'm not. I'm going HOME home! Heaven! Sit down and visit with me."

So they did, and shortly before midnight he lay back down and went home to be with the Lord.

Psalm 37:23 says: **The steps of a good man are ordered by the Lord: and he delighteth in his way.** Let your steps be ordered by the Lord as grandparents.

With our first book *Train Up a Child*, we had more grandparents buy the book than you might think. In fact, while sharing with a group in Fort Worth, Texas, a grandparent approached me in tears after one of the meetings on *Train Up a Child*. He gave me twenty dollars and told me to send him as many books as that would buy when it was published. (I didn't have any plans to do so at that time.) He said, "I'm getting the tapes of this meeting and give each child of mine a set. First I'm going to ask their forgiveness for not raising them according to the Word of God and pray they will follow God's way of training with my grandchildren." The mandate to train up your children in the way they should is not just to parents but to grandparents as well.

Don't Accept Defeat for Your Family

You have seen the portrait of the Christian home painted by the Word in Psalm 127 and 128. That is what God intends *your* home to look like. So don't give up on your family. Don't allow the devil to destroy what is precious in the sight of God.

The devil can't take charge of our city, our state or our nation unless he is allowed to carry out his evil strategies in our families. And he can't carry out his strategies in *your* home unless you have opened the gate and let him in!

There is so much for us to learn about being godly mothers and fathers. There is so much to learn about how to train our children in the way they should go. But in the midst of it all, we don't have to fret about the direction the world is going or the signs of the times. All we have to do is look unto Jesus and the Cross of Calvary. His blood was shed to deliver us and our families from the destruction that lies ahead.

Many people ignorantly accept every destructive thing that comes their way. They even seem to live each day of their lives expecting more destruction to come their way.

But we are the children of the Most High God. We should expect the best for our families, because God gave us His best — His Son Jesus.

So stay in tune with the Holy Ghost, with the Father God and with Jesus Christ. Let the Lord build your house as you trust in His power to meet your family's every need. Don't allow the devil to work destruction in your home anymore. Run him out in the name of Jesus, and you will see freedom come forth! Chains of bondage will become powerless under your feet.

You serve a mighty God, and He will always be there to guide and empower you as you seek to establish a godly home. So refuse to accept defeat. Expect nothing less than God's best for your family as you train up your children in the way they should go!

Prayer for Our Children

Father, we desire for our children to be godly and holy (Mal. 2:15). By faith we see them set apart unto God (1 Cor. 7:14). Our prayer is that they will complete all of their days on this earth (Isa. 65:23).

All of our house shall be saved (Acts 11:14), for all of our house shall believe in God (Acts 16:34). Our seed shall multiply on this earth (Gen. 22:17). We shall teach them effectively and train them responsibly as we talk with them and walk with them, and as they lie down and rise up (Deut. 6:7).

Our children shall possess their enemies' gates (Gen. 22:17; Gen. 24:60). We know our children are prized possessions of the Lord (Ps. 127:3). You have made them as arrows or weapons of defense for us (Ps. 127:4). They will be obedient children, obeying without objection.

Our children will answer God's call on their lives and be polished arrows in His quiver (Isa. 49:1-2). They shall be concealed weapons for God and His people all the days of their lives.

Why We Discipline

For I know him, that he will command his children and his household after him, and they shall keep the way of the LORD, to do justice and judgment; that the LORD may bring upon Abraham that which he hath spoken of him.

Genesis 18:19

O that there were such an heart in them, that they would fear me, and keep all my commandments always, that it might be well with them, and with their children for ever!

Deuteronomy 5:29

Observe and hear all these words which I command thee, that it may go well with thee, and with thy children after thee for ever, when thou doest that which is good and right in the sight of the Lord thy God.

Deuteronomy 12:28

He that spareth his rod hateth his son: but he that loveth him chasteneth him betimes.

Proverbs 13:24

Train up a child in the way he should go: and when he is old, he will not depart from it.

Proverbs 22:6

Foolishness is bound in the heart of a child; but the rod of correction shall drive it far from him.

Proverbs 22:15

Withhold not correction from the child: for if thou beatest him with the rod, he shall not die. Thou shalt beat him with the rod, and shalt deliver his soul from hell.

Proverbs 23:13,14

The rod and reproof give wisdom: but a child left to himself bringeth his mother to shame....Correct thy son, and he shall give thee rest; yea, he shall give delight unto thy soul.

Proverbs 29:15,17

Chasten thy son while there is hope, and let not thy soul spare for his crying.

Proverbs 19:18

The fear of the Lord is the beginning of knowledge: but fools despise wisdom and instruction.

Proverbs 1:7

It is good for a man that he bear the yoke in his youth.

Lamentations 3:27

As for God, his way is perfect; the word of the Lord is tried: he is a buckler to all them that trust in him.

2 Samuel 22:31

And I will walk at liberty: for I seek thy precepts....Before I was afflicted I went astray: but now I have kept thy word....It is good for me that I have been afflicted; that I might learn thy statutes....I know, O Lord, that thy judgments are right, and that thou in faithfulness hast afflicted me.

Psalm 119:45,67,71,75

For whom the Lord loveth he chasteneth, and scourgeth every son whom he receiveth. If ye endure chastening, God dealeth with you as with sons; for what son is he whom the father chasteneth not? But if ye be without chastisement, whereof all are partakers, then are ye bastards, and not sons. Furthermore we have had fathers of our flesh which corrected us, and we gave them reverence: shall we not much rather be in subjection unto the Father of spirits, and live? For they verily for a few days chastened us after their own pleasure; but he for our profit, that we might be partakers of his holiness. Now no chastening for the present seemeth to be joyous, but grievous: nevertheless afterward it yieldeth the peaceable fruit of righteousness unto them which are exercised thereby.

Hebrews 12:6-11

If we confess our sins, he is faithful and just to forgive us our sins, and to cleanse us from all unrighteousness.

1 John 1:9

And I will restore to you the years that the locust hath eaten, the cankerworm and the caterpiller, and the palmerworm, my great army which I sent among you. And ye shall eat in plenty, and be satisfied, and praise the name of the Lord your God, that hath dealt wondrously with you: and my people shall never be ashamed. And ye shall know that I am in the midst of Israel, and that I am the Lord your God, and none else: and my people shall never be ashamed.

Joel 2:25-27

Come, and let us return unto the Lord: for he hath torn, and he will heal us; he hath smitten, and he will bind us up.

Hosea 6:1

But ye shall receive power, after that the Holy Ghost is come upon you: and ye shall be witnesses unto me both in Jerusalem, and in all Judaea, and in Samaria, and unto the uttermost part of the earth.

Acts 1:8

For this child I prayed; and the Lord hath given me my petition which I asked of him: Therefore also I have lent him to the Lord; as long as he liveth he shall be lent to the Lord. And he worshipped the Lord there.

1 Samuel 1:27,28

And she vowed a vow, and said, O Lord of hosts, if thou wilt indeed look on the affliction of thine handmaid, and remember me, and not forget thine handmaid, but wilt give unto thine handmaid a man child, then I will give him unto the Lord all the days of his life, and there shall no razor come upon his head.

1 Samuel 1:11

By faith Moses, when he was born, was hid three months of his parents, because they saw he was a proper child; and they were not afraid of the king's commandment.

Hebrews 11:23

And all thy children shall be taught of the Lord; and great shall be the peace of thy children.

Isaiah 54:13

Lo, children are an heritage of the Lord: and the fruit of the womb is his reward.

Psalm 127:3

Outcome of Training

Whosoever therefore shall humble himself as this little child, the same is greatest in the kingdom of heaven.

Matthew 18:4

Children's children are the crown of old men; and the glory of children are their fathers.

Proverbs 17:6

Her children arise up, and call her blessed; her husband also, and he praiseth her.

Proverbs 31:28

The father of the righteous shall greatly rejoice: and he that begetteth a wise child shall have joy of him.

Proverbs 23:24

Correct thy son, and he shall give thee rest; yea, he shall give delight unto thy soul.

Proverbs 29:17

Behold, I will send you Elijah the prophet before the coming of the great and dreadful day of the Lord: And he shall turn the heart of the fathers to the children, and the heart of the children to their fathers, lest I come and smite the earth with a curse.

Malachi 4:5,6

But the angel said unto him, Fear not, Zacharias: for thy prayer is heard; and thy wife Elisabeth shall bear thee a son, and thou shalt call his name John. And thou shalt have joy and gladness; and many shall rejoice at his birth. For he shall be great in the sight of the Lord, and shall drink neither wine nor strong drink; and he shall be filled with the Holy Ghost, even from his mother's womb. And many of the children of Israel shall he turn to the Lord their God. And he shall go before him in the spirit and power of Elias, to turn the hearts of the fathers to the children, and the disobedient to the wisdom of the just; to make ready a people prepared for the Lord.

Luke 1:13-17

Scriptures to Children

My son, despise not the chastening of the Lord; neither be weary of his correction; For whom the Lord loveth he correcteth; even as a father the son in whom he delighteth.

Proverbs 3:11,12

Hear, ye children, the instruction of a father, and attend to know understanding.

Proverbs 4:1

My son, attend unto my wisdom, and bow thine ear to my understanding....Lest thou give thine honour unto others, and thy years unto the cruel....And say, How have I hated instruction, and my heart despised reproof.

Proverbs 5:1,9,12

Hearken unto thy father that begat thee, and despise not thy mother when she is old.

Proverbs 23:22

Let every soul be subject to the higher powers. For there is no power but of God: the powers that be are ordained of God. Whosoever therefore resisteth the power, resisteth the ordinance of God: and they that resist shall receive to themselves damnation.

Romans 13:1,2

Children, obey your parents in the Lord: for this is right.
Honour thy father and mother; which is the first commandment with promise; That it may be well with thee, and thou mayest live long on the earth. And, ye fathers, provoke not your children to wrath: but bring them up in the nurture and admonition of the Lord.

Ephesians 6:1-4

Children, obey your parents in all things: for this is well pleasing unto the Lord. Fathers, provoke not your children to anger, lest they be discouraged.

Colossians 3:20,21

And I set before the sons of the house of the Rechabites pots full of wine, and cups, and I said unto them, Drink ye wine. But they said, We will drink no wine: for Jonadab the son of Rechab our father commanded us, saying, Ye shall drink no wine, neither ye, nor your sons for ever.

Jeremiah 35:5,6

What Does God Want?

For the unbelieving husband is sanctified by the wife, and the unbelieving wife is sanctified by the husband: else were your children unclean; but now are they holy.

1 Corinthians 7:14

Yet ye say, Wherefore? Because the Lord hath been witness between thee and the wife of thy youth, against whom thou hast dealt treacherously: yet is she thy companion, and the wife of thy covenant. And did he not make one? Yet had he the residue of the spirit. And wherefore one? That he might seek a godly seed. Therefore take heed to your spirit, and let none deal treacherously against the wife of his youth.

Malachi 2:14,15

For, behold, I create new heavens and a new earth: and the former shall not be remembered, nor come into mind. But be ye glad and rejoice for ever in that which I create: for, behold, I create Jerusalem a rejoicing, and her people a joy. And I will rejoice in Jerusalem, and joy in my people: and the voice of weeping shall be no more heard in her, nor the voice of crying. There shall be no more thence an infant of days, nor an old man that hath not filled his days: for the child shall die an hundred years old; but the sinner being an hundred years old shall be accursed. And they shall build houses, and inhabit them; and they shall plant vineyards, and eat the fruit of them. They shall not build, and another inhabit; they shall not plant, and another eat: for as the days of a tree are the days of my people, and mine elect shall long enjoy the work of their hands. They shall not labour in vain, nor bring forth for trouble; for they are the seed of the blessed of the Lord, and their offspring with them. And it shall come to pass, that before they call, I will answer; and while they are yet speaking, I will hear. The wolf and the lamb shall feed together, and the lion shall eat straw like the bullock: and dust shall be the serpent's meat. They shall not hurt nor destroy in all my holy mountain, saith the Lord.

Isaiah 65:17-25

Verily I say unto you, Whatsoever ye shall bind on earth shall be bound in heaven: and whatsoever ye shall loose on earth shall be loosed in heaven.

Matthew 18:18

Children Who Were Not Trained

Now the sons of Eli were sons of Belial; they knew not the Lord.

1 Samuel 2:12

Now Eli was very old, and heard all that his sons did unto all Israel; and how they lay with the women that assembled at the door of the tabernacle of the congregation. And he said unto them, Why do ye such things? for I hear of your evil dealings by all this people. Nay, my sons; for it is no good report that I hear: ye make the Lord's people to transgress.

1 Samuel 2:22-24

Fruit of No Training

Wherefore kick ye at my sacrifice and at mine offering, which I have commanded in my habitation; and honourest thy sons above me, to make yourselves fat with the chiefest of all the offerings of Israel my people?

1 Samuel 2:29

For I have told him that I will judge his house for ever for the iniquity which he knoweth; because his sons made themselves vile, and he restrained them not.

1 Samuel 3:13

And yet for all that, when they be in the land of their enemies, I will not cast them away, neither will I abhor them, to destroy them utterly, and to break my covenant with them: for I am the Lord their God. But I will for their sakes remember the covenant of their ancestors whom I brought forth out of the land of Egypt in the sight of the heathen, that I might be their God: I am the Lord.

Leviticus 26:44,45

That this is a rebellious people, lying children, children that will not hear the law of the Lord.

Isaiah 30:9

For rebellion is as the sin of witchcraft, and stubbornness is as iniquity and idolatry. Because thou hast rejected the word of the Lord, he hath also rejected thee from being king.

1 Samuel 15:23

Whoso curseth his father or his mother, his lamp shall be put out in obscure darkness.

Proverbs 20:20

Hearken unto thy father that begat thee, and despise not thy mother when she is old.

Proverbs 23:22

For every one that curseth his father or his mother shall be surely put to death: he hath cursed his father or his mother; his blood shall be upon him.

Leviticus 20:9

The eye that mocketh at his father, and despiseth to obey his mother, the ravens of the valley shall pick it out, and the young eagles shall eat it.

Proverbs 30:17

He also that is slothful in his work is brother to him that is a great waster.

Proverbs 18:9

Looking diligently lest any man fail of the grace of God; lest any root of bitterness springing up trouble you, and thereby many be defiled.

Hebrews 12:15

These are murmerers, complainers, walking after their own lusts; and their mouth speaketh great swelling words, having men's persons in admiration because of advantage.

Jude 16

Be ye not unequally yoked together with unbelievers: for what fellowship hath righteousness with unrighteousness? and what communion hath light with darkness?

2 Corinthians 6:14

Prayer for Our Family

Father, we pray over our home, believing You for supernatural results as we stand firm on Your Word. We know that You are the One who must build our house individually and collectively. We believe You are bringing us as a family into unity for our own good, as well as for our church fellowship. As we bring our unified home to the fellowship, we in turn **H**elp **O**thers **M**inister **E**ffectively (H-O-M-E).

As parents, we realize what influences us influences our children. When You made a covenant with Noah, it affected his entire family. When You made a covenant with Abraham, it affected his entire family. Therefore, as we make a blood covenant with Jesus, that will affect our entire family as well. We recognize the importance of our children. We give priority to our children as prized possessions of the Lord.

We see our home as You see it, Father — a family ministering to families and "a ministry with the home at heart." The Father heart of God is involved with each of us in our home. We confess in our home that *none will be lost*! We ask You, Father, to give us the heathen for an inheritance in Jesus' name! Amen!

Scriptures for the Family

For whatsoever things were written aforetime were written for our learning, that we through patience and comfort of the scriptures might have hope.

Romans 15:4

Except the Lord build the house, they labour in vain that build it: except the Lord keep the city, the watchman waketh but in vain....It is vain for you to rise up early, to sit up late, to eat the bread of sorrows: for so he giveth his beloved sleep....Lo, children are an heritage of the Lord: and the fruit of the womb is his reward....As arrows are in the hand of a mighty man; so are children of the youth....Happy is the man that hath his quiver full of them: they shall not be ashamed, but they shall speak with the enemies in the gate.

Psalm 127

Blessed is every one that feareth the Lord; that walketh in his ways. For thou shalt eat the labour of thine hands: happy shalt thou be, and it shall be well with thee. Thy wife shall be as a fruitful vine by the sides of thine house: thy children like olive plants round about thy table. Behold, that thus shall the man be blessed that feareth the Lord. The Lord shall bless thee out of Zion: and thou shalt see the good of Jerusalem all the days of thy life....Yea, thou shalt see thy children's children, and peace upon Israel.

Psalm 128

That in blessing I will bless thee, and in multiplying I will multiply thy seed as the stars of the heaven, and as the sand which is upon the sea shore; and thy seed shall possess the gate of his enemies.

Genesis 22:17

But with thee will I establish my covenant; and thou shalt come into the ark, thou, and thy sons, and thy wife, and thy sons' wives with thee.

Genesis 6:18

And the Lord appeared unto Abram, and said, Unto thy seed will I give this land: and there builded he an altar unto the Lord, who appeared unto him.

Genesis 12:7

For all the land which thou seest, to thee will I give it, and to thy seed for ever.

Genesis 13:15

And I will establish my covenant between me and thee and thy seed after thee in their generations for an everlasting covenant, to be a God unto thee, and to thy seed after thee. And I will give unto thee, and to thy seed after thee, the land wherein thou art a stranger, all the land of Canaan, for an everlasting possession; and I will be their God.

Genesis 17:7,8

The just man walketh in his integrity: his children are blessed after him....Even a child is known by his doings, whether his work be pure, and whether it be right.

Proverbs 20:7,11

Even so it is not the will of your Father which is in heaven, that one of these little ones should perish.

Matthew 18:14

Then were there brought unto him little children, that he should put his hands on them, and pray: and the disciples rebuked them. But Jesus said, Suffer little children, and forbid them not, to come unto me: for of such is the kingdom of heaven. And he laid his hands on them, and departed thence.

Matthew 19:13-15

Then the word of the Lord came unto me, saying, Before I formed thee in the belly I knew thee; and before thou camest forth out of the womb I sanctified thee, and I ordained thee a prophet unto the nations.

Jeremiah 1:4,5

Behold, I will send you Elijah the prophet before the coming of the great and dreadful day of the Lord: And he shall turn the heart of the fathers to the children, and the heart of the children to their fathers, lest I come and smite the earth with a curse.

Malachi 4:5,6

But the angel said unto him, Fear not, Zacharias: for thy prayer is heard; and thy wife Elisabeth shall bear thee a son, and thou shalt call his name John. And thou shalt have joy and gladness; and many shall rejoice at his birth. For he shall be great in the sight of the Lord, and shall drink neither wine nor strong drink; and he shall be filled with the Holy Ghost, even from his mother's womb. And many of the children of Israel shall he turn to the Lord their God. And he shall go before him in the spirit and power of Elias, to turn the hearts of the fathers to the children, and the disobedient to the wisdom of the just; to make ready a people prepared for the Lord.

Luke 1:13-17

At the same time came the disciples unto Jesus, saying, Who is the greatest in the kingdom of heaven? And Jesus called a little child unto him, and set him in the midst of them, And said, Verily I say unto you, Except ye be converted, and become as little children, ye shall not enter into the kingdom of heaven. Whosoever therefore shall humble himself as this little child, the same is greatest in the kingdom of heaven. And whoso shall receive one such little child in my name receiveth me. But whoso shall offend one of these little ones which believe in me, it were better for him that a millstone were hanged about his neck, and that he were drowned in the depth of the sea.

Matthew 18:1-6

Take heed that ye despise not one of these little ones; for I say unto you, That in heaven their angels do always behold the face of my Father which is in heaven....Even so it is not the will of your Father which is in heaven, that one of these little ones should perish.

Matthew 18:10,14

About the Author

Chuck Sturgeon, from Enid, Oklahoma, currently travels throughout the United States. He has shared the Word of God in ministry for the past 27 years. He is an author and speaker who shares in a simple and practical manner scriptural principles from the Word of God.

He and his wife Dea are called of God to minister to couples and families. They have practical knowledge and scriptural principles on the family to share with teens, parents and grandparents. Their messages will move you from laughter to tears and leave you with a peace knowing that God has answers for your family. Their story of how the Lord delivered Chuck from alcohol, saved them, filled them with the Holy Spirit and restored their marriage, is a powerful testimony of the goodness of our Father God. They have ministered as a team in seminars, campmeetings, revivals and crusades across the United States and Canada. Chuck and Dea minister with a humorous flavor and a special anointing in the area of marriage and family.

To contact Chuck Sturgeon, write:

Chuck Sturgeon
P. O. Box 904
Enid, Oklahoma 73702-0904

Please include your prayer requests
and comments when you write.

Additional copies of this book
are available from your local bookstore.

HARRISON HOUSE
Tulsa, Oklahoma 74153

The Harrison House Vision

Proclaiming the truth and the power

Of the Gospel of Jesus Christ

With excellence;

Challenging Christians to

Live victoriously,

Grow spiritually,

Know God intimately.